Conquering Challenges

KICKING CANCER WITH CHRIST

ELIZABETH C. JENKINS

WESTBOW
PRESS®
A DIVISION OF THOMAS NELSON
& ZONDERVAN

This book is a work of non-fiction. Unless otherwise noted, the author and the publisher make no explicit guarantees as to the accuracy of the information contained in this book and in some cases, names of people and places have been altered to protect their privacy.

WestBow Press books may be ordered through booksellers or by contacting:

WestBow Press
A Division of Thomas Nelson & Zondervan
1663 Liberty Drive
Bloomington, IN 47403
www.westbowpress.com
1 (866) 928-1240

Because of the dynamic nature of the Internet, any web addresses or links contained in this book may have changed since publication and may no longer be valid. The views expressed in this work are solely those of the author and do not necessarily reflect the views of the publisher, and the publisher hereby disclaims any responsibility for them.

Any people depicted in stock imagery provided by Getty Images are models, and such images are being used for illustrative purposes only.
Certain stock imagery © Getty Images.

Scripture quotations marked (NIV) are taken from the Holy Bible, New International Version®, NIV®. Copyright © 1973, 1978, 1984, 2011 by Biblica, Inc.™ Used by permission of Zondervan. All rights reserved worldwide. www.zondervan.com The "NIV" and "New International Version" are trademarks registered in the United States Patent and Trademark Office by Biblica, Inc.™

Scripture quotations marked MSG are taken from THE MESSAGE, copyright © 1993, 2002, 2018 by Eugene H. Peterson. Used by permission of NavPress. All rights reserved. Represented by Tyndale House Publishers, Inc.

Scripture quotations marked (NLT) are taken from the Holy Bible, New Living Translation, copyright ©1996, 2004, 2015 by Tyndale House Foundation. Used by permission of Tyndale House Publishers, Inc., Carol Stream, Illinois 60188. All rights reserved.

ISBN: 978-1-9736-6135-1 (sc)
ISBN: 978-1-9736-6137-5 (hc)
ISBN: 978-1-9736-6136-8 (e)

Library of Congress Control Number: 2019905248

Print information available on the last page.

WestBow Press rev. date: 5/22/2019

January 1

Tell everyone who is discouraged, Be strong and don't be afraid! God is coming to your rescue.
—Isaiah 35:4

I have to admit this is one area I still need to grow in. Does this make me a bad person? I don't know. I think it makes me an honest person. When I ask is there anything I can do or call me anytime? I mean it, but I hope they don't ask too much of me.

I ask because I feel in my heart this is what God wants me to do. I am willing. He knows I will do it too. God is coming to my rescue and the other person's too.

January 2

Do not worry about your life, what you will eat; or about your body, what you will wear. Life is more than food, and the body more than clothes. Consider the ravens: They do not sow or reap, they have no storeroom or barn; yet God feeds them. And how much more valuable you are than birds! Who of you by worrying can add a single hour to his life? Since you cannot do this very little thing, why do you worry about the rest?
—Luke 12:22-26

There was a time in my life I thought, "How am I going to pay my bills? How would I take care of my child? What was I going to drive?"

I was trapped in a corner. I had no choice but to rely on God. It did work out. The bills were always paid on time. I received a check in the mail and used it to make a down payment on a car. I applied for food stamps. I received a raise at work, and I got off the food stamps. We were always provided with what we needed.

I saw the love of God working through other people. It was a very valuable and concrete message for me. I also realized sometimes I have to go through something for other people to learn lessons too.

January 3

The Lord is my light and my salvation—whom shall I fear? The Lord is the stronghold of my life—of whom shall I be afraid?
—PSALM 27:1

I have experienced fear at a level I didn't even know possible. I had to face my mortality more than once in my lifetime. Looking back, this was when I had a major shift in my thinking.

It was a time I realized my utter powerlessness, and there was nothing but to believe in God. When I got to this point my fear dissipated. I finally gave up trying to solve the problem, and I turned it over to God. The fear left, and the solution came.

*Cast your cares on the Lord and he will sustain
you; he will never let the righteous fall.*
—PSALM 55:22

When I was diagnosed with cancer I wondered, "How long would I live? I didn't want to die. I would miss my children. I was too young to die. Would my kids be alright?"

Memories from the past flooded my mind. It was like watching a movie, and I couldn't put it on pause. I kept hitting rewind and play.

Finally, I'd had enough. I wrote all my cares and worries down and put them in my God box. I could feel myself letting the issues go.

God's got this!

January 5

Immediately he spoke to them and said, "Take courage! It is I. Don't be afraid."
—MARK 6:50

Courage isn't the absence of fear. It's the ability to walk through the fear in spite of it. I was letting fear rule my life.

I read when Jesus was in the garden, and knew he was going to die. He had tremendous fear. Even though it was a great outcome for all. To me this is a great example of courage.

When I found out I had cancer I would be lying if I said I wasn't afraid. Since I had the same cancer as my father, I had only the experience of what he went through battling it before it took his life.

Fear still comes back full force out of nowhere. I have to summon all the courage I have and continue to walk through the fears—not above, below, or around them.

January 6

"For I am the Lord, your God, who takes hold of your
right hand and says to you, Do not fear; I will help you.
Do not be afraid, for I myself will help you," declares
"the Lord, your Redeemer, the Holy One of Israel."
—Isaiah 41:13-14

When my children were scared. I held their hands or them until they felt safe. My children would get a boo-boo. They came running to me. I kissed it and made it feel better. I securely held them and told them they would be alright. I bandaged their wounds.

This is what God does for me and you.

January 7

Fear of man will prove to be a snare, but
whoever trusts in the Lord is kept safe.
—PROVERBS 29:25

I believe God puts people in my life who walk with me and teach me courage. There comes a time when it is just God and me. I can depend on God for the strength and courage to walk me through the fear.

I have grown the most spiritually during these times.

He got up, rebuked the wind and said to the waves, "Quiet! Be still!"
Then the wind died down and it was completely calm. He said to
his disciples, "Why are you so afraid? Do you still have no faith?"
—MARK 4:39-40

I remember a time I was driving back home. The usual route was closed. I had to go a way I hadn't been before. I called my brother because my fear level was escalating.

I had stopped my car in the middle of a country road. A man rapped on my window. I rolled it down. He asked if I was alright.

I told him frantically, "I'm trying to get to Nolensville Road, and I don't know how to get there."

He pointed in the direction I was going and told me to continue to go straight. I thanked him, and he went back to his car. Later, I thought about this and thought he had to be an angel. There was no other explanation. He appeared out of nowhere.

When God knows I need help he always comes through.

January 9

*The angel of the Lord encamps around those
who fear him, and he delivers them.*
—PSALM 34:7

I have a deep respect and reverence for God, and I am still in awe of Him.

My God has already delivered me from so many situations that weren't good for my spiritual growth along with many physical ailments.

Why wouldn't he now?

January 10

But even if you suffer for doing what is right, God will reward
you for it. So don't worry or be afraid of their threats.
—1 Peter 3:14

While I was growing up my dad and mom managed their money very well. Others would come for their financial advice. They usually followed it for a little while, and, eventually, the temptation of material things would take hold.

I was in my early 30s before I began living financially responsible. My parents became an example to me. I asked them questions and took their advice.

The same is true watching people live with cancer. I have watched how they have lived with cancer—their courage; their attitudes; their actions; their strength; their ups and downs; their sense of humor; or their acceptance, if they receive a new cancer diagnosis.

January 11

I prayed to the Lord, and he answered me.
He freed me from all my fears.
—Psalm 34:4

When I finally give everything to God a peace washes over me. It is one of the greatest freedoms I have the privilege of experiencing. It is better than anything else I have used to try and fix my feelings. The fear disappears, and I know deep in my being that all will be well within and outside of me.

January 12

Do not be afraid of them; the Lord your
God himself will fight for you.
—DEUTERONOMY 3:22

There have been times in my life when I know with utmost certainty that God is there for me. He is fighting my battles along with Jesus, the Holy Spirit, and the angels. He fights my seen and unseen battles.

I remember one time when I was out of town. I was shouting out loud in the parking lot. "I pray for the protection of the holy and guardian angels."

The person I was with told me I was crazy. No harm came to us. I wasn't called crazy any more.

January 13

The Word became flesh and made his dwelling among us.
We have seen his glory, the glory of the one and only Son,
who came from the Father, full of grace and truth.
—JOHN 1:14

Thank God for Jesus. He is my Advocate, My Intercessor, and My Healer. He is in the miracle and healing business.

Jesus told him, "Don't be afraid; just believe."
—MARK 5:36

Sometimes this is easier said than done. When I believe to the bottom of my core it's easy not to be afraid.

I remember when I had been trying on my own to quit drinking and drugging, and it wasn't working. I finally gave up and turned it over to God. I knew deep down he had taken care of this for me, and I wasn't afraid any longer.

The same is true for anything I go through. I just have to believe that God does exist, and some things I can't explain or define. I just know them to be true because of the results.

January 15

The Lord your God is in your midst, A victorious warrior.
He will exult over you with joy, He will be quiet in His
love, He will rejoice over you with shouts of joy.
—Zephaniah 3:17

I might not physically see him. Sometimes I might feel his presence, and sometimes I may not. God is always there for me and you.

January 16

He who dwells in the shelter of the Most High will rest in
the shadow of the Almighty. I will say of the Lord, "He is
my refuge and my fortress, my God, in whom I trust."
—Psalm 91:1-2

God is my protector. He sends his angels to protect me either visibly or invisibly. If I am aware, it's a feeling that rushes over and through me. I can remember four times in my life when I experienced their presence.

I still have my doubts. I just keep living my life praying and trying not to pay attention to my thoughts, doubts, and fears. Once through the experience my faith grows.

January 17

Heal me, O Lord, and I will be healed; save me and
I will be saved, for you are the one I praise.
—JEREMIAH 17:14

God is healing me from the cancer. My hip tumor and groin lymph nodes are nonexistent, and there are no new malignant tumors in my brain. My lung tumor is shrinking and not active.

I imagine God and my guardian angels healing me every day. Why? I have turned it over to God. I just show up for the treatments letting God work through my doctors, the oncologists, radiologist, surgeons, technicians, and nurses.

January 18

Worship the LORD your God, and his blessing will be on your
food and water. I will take away sickness from among you.
—EXODUS 23:25

I felt I had a pretty good relationship with God—reading my mediations, journaling, praying, and mediating. I then found out I had cancer. I told my friends. "I guess God wants more of my attention."

I read this scripture every day. I know in my core God will heal me. His intended purpose for me hasn't been fulfilled.

I breathe in God's love, and his healing. I breathe out my fears and the disease.

January 19

Surely he took up our pain and bore our suffering, yet we considered him punished by God, stricken by him, and afflicted. But he was pierced for our transgressions, he was crushed for our iniquities; the punishment that brought us peace was on him, and by his wounds we are healed.
—Isaiah 53:4-5

God came to earth in human form to die for my sins. He saved me from myself. I couldn't understand this concept.

It took my cancer diagnosis to comprehend just how much God loves me.

I would do the same for my children. I would do anything to save them, their souls, their future, their everything. I would die for them.

*"But I will restore you to health and heal
your wounds," declares the LORD.*
—Jeremiah 30:17

I went to my oncologist yesterday. He told me he was surprised. My cancer was inactive. I was in shock myself.

I said to him, "You said for me to be prepared to begin treatments in February."

He replied, "Yes, I did, but nothing is active. This was more than I had hoped for."

"I guess the mediations I have been doing are working."

"Yes, I am sure it doesn't hurt, just keep doing it."

Why? Because God works.

January 21

You restored me to health and let me live. Surely it was for my benefit that I suffered such anguish. In your love you kept me from the pit of destruction; you have put all my sins behind your back.
—ISAIAH 38:16-17

I knew deep in my soul I was to write. I found out I had cancer, and I began writing about my experiences. It evolved into a daily meditation book for people with cancer, or any disease one has to live with day to day.

If this book helps one person, it will be worth everything I have already gone through.

January 22

"I have seen their ways, but I will heal them; I will guide them and restore comfort to Israel's mourners, creating praise on their lips. Peace, peace, to those far and near," says the LORD. "And I will heal them."
—Isaiah 57:18-19

I turned from God in my middle school years. I was angry at him for allowing circumstances to happen to me during my childhood. I was a fearful person, and I felt unattractive and unloved.

I finally hit bottom and looked over my life. I realized God was the only answer. I turned everything over to him, and I had a peace come over me that was indescribable. I praise him for taking away that problem along with many others.

Cancer then entered my body. After much distress, crying, morbid thoughts, regrets, and forgiveness I finally turned this over to God. He is the only one who has the ultimate power to heal me.

January 23

Nevertheless, I will bring health and healing to it; I will heal my
people and will let them enjoy abundant peace and security.
—JEREMIAH 33:6

God is healing my body. I am getting stronger and can breathe better day by day. It is only because of God, Jesus Christ, and the Holy Spirit that this is possible.

January 24

Dear friend, I pray that you may enjoy good health and that all may go well with you, even as your soul is getting along well.
—3 JOHN 1:2

I really don't know what is good or bad for me. I was diagnosed with cancer. I didn't realize how many friends I had, and how good people could be. They brought food over, gave me rides to treatments, listened to me, and sat with me. There is nothing like a good friend to support you during good and bad times.

These actions nourished my soul along with my health. My belief that God works through others was strengthened.

January 25

And my God will meet all your needs according
to the riches of his glory in Christ Jesus.
—Philippians 4:19

This scripture says all my needs, not some of my needs will be met. God has gotten me through anaphylactic shock, overdoses, and colon polyps taken out before they became cancerous.

He is now with me through the lung cancer. He is healing me. He isn't finished with me yet. He still has work for me to do.

January 26

My son, pay attention to what I say; turn your ear to my words.
Do not let them out of your sight, keep them within your heart; for
they are life to those who find them and health to one's whole body.
—PROVERBS 4:20-22

When I found out I had cancer I had to enlarge my relationship with God in order to get through the day. I began writing anything spiritual that touched my soul. While in my car I would listen to spiritual Podcasts filling my head with God's word instead of Satan's.

I would quote scriptures when attacked by negative thinking. My mediations became more personal. I learned to ask for help from others and from God.

These actions were setting spiritual concrete into my being.

January 27

A cheerful heart is good medicine, but a
crushed spirit dries up the bones.
—PROVERBS 7:22

I notice when I compliment or praise other people's actions they just beam. This also works for me. I feel better when I think or say out loud positive words about myself rather than negative ones.

January 28

There is a time for everything, and a season for every activity under the heavens: a time to be born and a time to die, a time to plant and a time to uproot, a time to kill and a time to heal, a time to tear down and a time to build, a time to weep and a time to laugh, a time to mourn and a time to dance, a time to scatter stones and a time to gather them, a time to embrace and a time to refrain from embracing, a time to search and a time to give up, a time to keep and a time to throw away, a time to tear and a time to mend, a time to be silent and a time to speak, a time to love and a time to hate, a time for war and a time for peace.
—ECCLESIASTES 3:1-8

Life isn't always candy and gumdrops. Sometimes it's persimmons and spoiled milk. Either way, God is in charge. I tell people God is going to have his way.

I have learned there is no use fighting or struggling. I know ultimately it is for my good because this has been my experience. It doesn't mean I don't still struggle. I just don't do it as long as I used too.

January 29

LORD, be gracious to us; we long for you. Be our strength every morning, our salvation in time of distress.
—Isaiah 33:2

God is with me every day. I know this in my heart. It doesn't mean I always feel it.

God has been the one to get me through many ailments, diseases, and fears. He gave me the strength to get through my distress. I do know this as sure as I am breathing.

January 30

Therefore confess your sins to each other and pray
for each other so that you may be healed. The prayer
of a righteous person is powerful and effective.
—James 5:6

There is power in confessing one's sins. It's such a release. I feel the negativity, sickness, and the darkness leave me. I feel lighter and more joyful.

Before I would cover up my feelings of guilt, fear, and inferiority with various actions that didn't work. It would take days or weeks before I would talk with someone about my shortcomings. Now, it might take a day, a few hours, or a few minutes before I make a call or talk with someone in person.

I have experienced the power of prayer. I have had people tell me they have been praying for me, and I didn't even know it. Their prayers worked.

January 31

He himself bore our sins in his body on the cross, so
that we might die to sins and live for righteousness;
by his wounds you have been healed.
—1 PETER 2:24

Jesus has healed me of my many afflictions. Why? Because he loves me as well as you.

February 1

Come to me, all you who are weary and burdened, and I will give you rest. Take my yoke upon you and learn from me, for I am gentle and humble in heart, and you will find rest for your souls.
—MATTHEW 11:28-29

I have seen people carrying or pulling an item that is way too heavy for them. They insist on doing it anyway. They don't ask for help. Only when they ask for help. The load is shared, and it becomes easier to handle.

I have been guilty of this. It can sometimes still be hard to ask for help. When I do it is much easier to handle the load.

When I ask Jesus for help I am lighter and freer.

February 2

He gives strength to the weary and increases the power of the weak.
—Isaiah 40:29

When I am at my weakest God is at his strongest. When all doors, windows, and blinds have been closed God's door is wide open. He is waiting for me to ask for his help, his will, his action plan. I then become strong. God gives me the power for anything coming my way.

February 3

No temptation has overtaken you except what is common to mankind. And God is faithful; he will not let you be tempted beyond what you can bear. But when you are tempted, he will also provide a way out so that you can endure it.
—1 CORINTHIANS 10:13

God hasn't failed me when I cry for his help.

When I encounter a temptation it's because I am not satisfied with how things are currently going in my life. I think this temptation will fix the problem.

It might work for a few seconds, days, weeks, or months. It will wreck not only my life, but also many other people in my life. This causes more dissatisfaction.

When the temptation becomes too much for me, and I know I am headed for trouble. I ask God for his help confessing I can't do it on my own. It has been through much heartache I ask God for help more readily. I don't want to experience the remorse, guilt, and distrust of others.

February 4

*Then they cried to the LORD in their trouble, and he
saved them from their distress. He sent out his word
and healed them; he rescued them from the grave.*
—PSALM 107:19-20

God is good. God knew when I had enough. He knew when I
surrendered.

I knew. I could feel it in my mind, body, and spirit. I knew all would
be well.

February 5

LORD my God, I called to you for help, and you healed me.
—Psalm 30:2

This is so true. It's when I cried, yelled, and pleaded for God to help me is when the healing began. He is a healing and loving God. He sent his Son to show us how loving and healing he continues to be.

February 6

Have mercy on me, LORD, for I am faint; heal
me, LORD, for my bones are in agony.
—PSALM 6:2

By the time I found out I had lung cancer it had spread to my hip bone. My hip and leg were literally in agony. They had to do a hip stabilization surgery. They were afraid my hip would fracture before I completed radiation. I knew God was the only one who would be able to heal me through the doctors, nurses, surgeons, radiologists, and technicians.

Seven months later my hip doesn't hurt anything like it did. There are times it doesn't hurt at all. My lung cancer is now in remission.

The LORD protects and preserves them— they are counted among the blessed in the land - he does not give them over to the desire of their foes. The LORD sustains them on their sickbed and restores them from their bed of illness.
—PSALM 41:2-3

Many diseases have tried to kill me either spiritually, physically, or mentally. I have cried to the Lord, and he hasn't failed me.

The restoration might not be on my timetable. It might be a slow and sometimes painful process. It does come, and sometimes against all odds.

February 8

I said, "Have mercy on me, LORD; heal
me, for I have sinned against you."
—PSALM 41:4

Have I sinned? Yes.

There have been times I did things that I knew weren't good for my body even before I began doing them.

I did these things for years and then gave them up. It doesn't give me immunity from still facing the repercussions of my actions. This is when the above scripture becomes pertinent in my life.

February 9

*Hear, LORD, and be merciful to me; LORD, be
my help. You turned my wailing into dancing; you
removed my sackcloth and clothed me with joy.*
—PSALM 30:10-11

If I got what I deserved, I wouldn't be sitting here writing this mediation book. I would be either dead, in jail, or still in a mental, physical, and spiritual torment. God heard my wailing, and, now, I am dancing. God is merciful to me.

February 10

My flesh and my heart may fail, but God is the
strength of my heart and my portion forever.
—PSALM 73:26

No matter what happens to my body or mind—God is there through it all. When life gets tough facing adversities I remember God has sacrificed himself. He has given me a portion of himself. He has promised me a portion of heaven.

February 11

*On hearing this, Jesus said to them, "It is not the
healthy who need a doctor, but the sick. I have not
come to call the righteous, but sinners."*
—MARK 2:17

People who think they are well don't believe they need help. I tried running my life. I made a complete and utter mess of it.

I realized I couldn't go on this way. I was a sick person. I wasn't quite sure God would help. I read this verse, and I realized God would be my doctor. I began to get better, and I recovered slowly.

February 12

Jesus went through all the towns and villages, teaching
in their synagogues, proclaiming the good news of the
kingdom and healing every disease and sickness.
—MATTHEW 9:35

Jesus' healing spirit is working through the doctors, nurses, and others. He is healing me from the cancer that is trying to take over my body. Jesus is the source. He has the power.

Through Jesus my disease is being eradicated. I am sharing my experience, strength, and hope of the power of Jesus. He uses me to relay to others how to live a full and joyful life with cancer.

February 13

When Jesus saw her, he called her forward and said to her, "Woman, you are set free from your infirmity." Then he put his hands on her, and immediately she straightened up and praised God.
—LUKE 13:12-13

The Lord set her free. He is in the miracle and healing business. If he did it for her, why not me or you?

February 14

Stretch out your hand to heal and perform signs and wonders through the name of your holy servant Jesus. After they prayed, the place where they were meeting was shaken. And they were all filled with the Holy Spirit and spoke the word of God boldly.
—Acts 4:30-31

I need God, Jesus Christ, and the Holy Spirit to be completely centered, whole, and grounded. The trinity has allowed me to live life on this earth while others see the miracles in my life.

February 15

*There he found a man named Aeneas, who was paralyzed
and had been bedridden for eight years. "Aeneas,"
Peter said to him, "Jesus Christ heals you. Get up and
roll up your mat." Immediately Aeneas got up.*
—ACTS 9:33-34

God has the power to heal me in all areas of my life. As a friend once told me, "Sometimes I need God with skin on it."

When I know another person is praying for me this is uplifting. If they believe he has the power to heal me, it increases my faith.

There is also power in numbers. When I falter there is someone there to pick me up physically, spiritually, mentally, or emotionally.

February 16

You know what has happened throughout the province of Judea,
beginning in Galilee after the baptism that John preached - how
God anointed Jesus of Nazareth with the Holy Spirit and power,
and how he went around doing good and healing all who were
under the power of the devil, because God was with him.
—Acts 10:37-38

God is with me. I might not always feel it, but deep down I "know" it. I have to act as if God is with me and for me. I have to remember not to beat myself up when I have doubts.

Jesus knew he was going to die and be with his Father. He still had doubts. He was scared, frightened, and angry with his disciples.

Why wouldn't I have doubts? My friends and family are for me in this life. God is with me through this life journey as well as the next one.

Simon's mother-in-law was in bed with a fever, and they immediately told Jesus about her. So he went to her, took her hand and helped her up. The fever left her and she began to wait on them.
—MARK 1:29-31

Jesus still performs miracles today. I am a miracle. Jesus is still in the healing and miracle business.

February 18

While Jesus was still speaking, someone came from the house of Jairus, the synagogue leader. "Your daughter is dead," he said. "Don't bother the teacher anymore." Hearing this, Jesus said to Jairus, "Don't be afraid; just believe, and she will be healed." When he arrived at the house of Jairus, he did not let anyone go in with him except Peter, John and James, and the child's father and mother. Meanwhile, all the people were wailing and mourning for her. "Stop wailing," Jesus said. "She is not dead but asleep." They laughed at him, knowing that she was dead. But he took her by the hand and said, "My child, get up!" Her spirit returned, and at once she stood up. Then Jesus told them to give her something to eat.
—LUKE 8:49-55

An important fact in this scripture, "Then Jesus told them to give her something to eat."

I was in the hospital for five days with pneumonia and pleurisy. My husband came to take me home. Getting out of the car and going into the house took all of the energy I had.

Everyday my husband took me to a restaurant that served home-cooked meals. I became stronger with each passing day until I was completely healed.

February 19

For he has rescued us from the dominion of darkness
and brought us into the kingdom of the Son he loves, in
whom we have redemption, the forgiveness of sins.
—COLOSSIANS 1:13-14

I found out I had cancer. I was in a darkness I couldn't get out of without God's help.

I accepted I had cancer; I would have a hip stabilization; I would have radiation, chemotherapy, and immunotherapy treatments; I would have groin lymph nodes removed; I would have two brain tumors extracted; and I would have side effects—mental, physical, spiritual, and emotional.

Did I do this readily? Hardly. I kicked, screamed, and pleaded until finally I gave God the darkness. He redeemed me and brought me into the light.

February 20

Three times I pleaded with the Lord to take it away from me. But he said to me, "My grace is sufficient for you, for my power is made perfect in weakness." Therefore I will boast all the more gladly about my weaknesses, so that Christ's power may rest on me.
—2 CORINTHIANS 12:8-9

It wasn't until I absolutely gave up, and utterly surrendered my life to God when things turned around for me. I have seen many others giving up their addictions to God, and he led them to the answers.

February 21

We are hard pressed on every side, but not crushed;
perplexed, but not in despair; persecuted, but not
abandoned; struck down, but not destroyed.
—2 CORINTHIANS 4:8-9

I know God has my back. I feel all these feelings, and I will continue to do so since I am human. I do know in the core of my being that God is on my side.

February 22

I will give you a new heart and put a new spirit in you; I will
remove from you your heart of stone and give you a heart of flesh.
—EZEKIEL 36:26

During different periods of my life my heart has been full of resentment, fear, bitterness, despair, and other negative emotions. They had control of me, and my decisions were based on them. I realized I had to give up those emotions. They were holding me back. My heart was replaced with love, peace, faith, and joy.

February 23

I have been crucified with Christ and I no longer live, but Christ lives in me. The life I now live in the body, I live by faith in the Son of God, who loved me and gave himself for me.
—GALATIANS 2:20

I know that my life was saved by Jesus Christ when he was crucified. My sins were crucified at the same time. They died. I wasn't bound. I realized the depth that Jesus' and God's love went, and I was willing to live in faith.

I give them eternal life, and they shall never perish; no one will snatch them out of my hand. My Father, who has given them to me, is greater than all; no one can snatch them out of my Father's hand.
—John 10:28-29

God and Jesus have me. I know this in my head. I have eternal life, but I don't always believe or feel it. In my core I know it's true.

February 25

and teaching them to obey everything I have commanded you.
And surely I am with you always, to the very end of the age.
—MATTHEW 28:20

This gives me comfort. I have someone walking through this life with me along with the next.

February 26

Do not forsake wisdom, and she will protect you;
love her, and she will watch over you.
—PROVERBS 4:6

I wished I had listened to the voice deep inside my soul before taking an action. I suffered the consequences in hurting others or myself by not listening. Also, I haven't adhered to the wisdom or experience of others, and I paid dearly for this.

Now, I am older, and I am more readily to listen to my inner voice or the wisdom of others before I act. The outcome is much more agreeable.

February 27

Discretion will protect you, and understanding will guard you.
—PROVERBS 2:11

I don't know how many times I acted on my emotions. This didn't do me any good at all, and at times made relationships with others irreparable.

Someone told me people were doing the best they could. An example I was given. If someone passed me on the road or cut me off, it's doesn't necessarily have anything to do with me. They could be driving to the hospital because someone was in a wreck, or they had a sick child in the car.

I was willing to give myself many breaks, but not others.

It was suggested I needed to make excuses for others.

February 28

But let all who take refuge in you be glad; let them ever sing for joy. Spread your protection over them, that those who love your name may rejoice in you.
—PSALM 5:11

I know in my head God will protect me; he is my refuge; and he has the wings to protect me and others. I don't always believe it.

It's only when I have tried all my ways that I go to my Father— defeated, broken, and afraid. I don't even have to say a word or ask him anything. He is always there waiting to spread his wings over me. I don't have to hurt any longer.

I then have the strength to go back out into the world.

February 29

"Because the poor are plundered and the needy
groan, I will now arise," says the Lord. "I will
protect them from those who malign them."
—PSALM 12:5

Someone told me many years ago life isn't fair. My God is. He knows what is best for me even though I might not understand it. He is always there to protect me. The hardest thing for me to do is nothing when my reputation is being attacked. I know the truth will prevail in the end.

March 1

May the LORD answer you when you are in distress;
may the name of the God of Jacob protect you.
—PSALM 20:1

God has always answered my prayers. They are always to my benefit. I might not see it immediately, but eventually I do. The true test of my faith is when some answers aren't revealed until the hereafter.

March 2

The righteous person may have many troubles,
but the LORD delivers him from them all.
—Psalm 34:19

I was diagnosed with stage IV lung cancer. It had metastasized to my hip, which was almost fractured. I had to get a hip stabilization and titanium rod before I could receive any treatments.

Over the next one-and-a-half years the cancer spread to my lymph nodes and brain. The malignant nodes and tumors were removed. I am now receiving immunotherapy every three weeks.

Who is delivering me? The Lord.

March 3

*Have mercy on me, my God, have mercy on me, for
in you I take refuge. I will take refuge in the shadow
of your wings until the disaster has passed.*
—PSALM 57:1

My God has mercy on me even when I don't ask. He has protected me from many situations, which weren't good for me. He has shown me how much he cares and loves me.

March 4

Deliver me from my enemies, O God; be my
fortress against those who are attacking me.
—Psalm 59:1

I have enemies I can see. I also have enemies that are unseen, such as evil spirits, physical and mental diseases, and fears. God sends his angels to surround me so nothing can penetrate or reach me.

March 5

Though I walk in the midst of trouble, you preserve
my life. You stretch out your hand against the anger
of my foes; with your right hand you save me.
—PSALM 138:7

I was driving while intoxicated. I was approaching a bridge, but I was seeing two. I looked over at my passenger seat, and there was a spirit sitting there pointing at which bridge I should take. God reached out his hand to save me.

Keep me safe, LORD, from the hands of the wicked; protect
me from the violent, who devise ways to trip my feet.
—PSALM 140:4

God is my vindicator. He is always on alert for my safety. I have known when people were against me, and I haven't even had a clue when someone intended to harm me. God is always making sure I am safe.

March 7

The Lord is good to all; he has compassion on all he has made.
—PSALM 145:9

I know people who have killed others while drunk driving, have served time in prison, or have broken up marriages. They turned their lives over to Christ, and they became different people.

When I turned my life over to Christ my life and relationships began to get better. I now know God has a plan for me, which is going to show his power and mercy. He has the power to heal my diseases.

God has compassion for you and me.

March 8

The Lord will keep you from all harm — he will watch over your life; the Lord will watch over your coming and going both now and forevermore.
—Psalm 121:7-8

I always had the Lord watching over me. I can look back and see many instances he kept me from harm. Others attempting to retaliate for my actions against them, or others trying to harm me for no reason.

March 9

My God is my rock, in whom I take refuge, my shield and
the horn of my salvation. He is my stronghold, my refuge
and my savior— from violent people you save me.
—2 SAMUEL 22:3

When there is nothing left but to depend on God. He becomes my boulder. He keeps me centered. I do try to rely on others for comfort, assurance, and understanding, but another person can only do so much. God is my source. He is my protector. I go to God quicker than in my past. I know he is always on my side.

March 10

But if Christ is in you, then even though your body is subject to death because of sin, the Spirit gives life because of righteousness.
—ROMANS 8:10

My body began dying the moment I was born. I only have so much time because of the sins I committed, and the future ones yet to commit. I am a work in progress. I have been saved, and my spirit will live.

I was diagnosed with cancer, and my life took on a deeper meaning. I knew God wasn't finished with me yet.

God has a mission for me. One I have put off for years. He wants me to share my experience, strength, and hope. Others will then know the power of his love, strength, grace, compassion, and mercy.

March 11

But the Lord is faithful, and he will strengthen
you and protect you from the evil one.
—2 Thessalonians 3:3

Satan attempts to attack me every day. Some days are easier than others resisting his wily ways. He is tricky and deceitful, but God is my source. God is the one who has the power to strengthen and protect me from the evil one.

God has given me tools to fight the daily battle. Some of the tools include The Bible; God; Jesus Christ; the Holy Spirit; angels; family, friends, and strangers; journaling; reading the experience of others; and listening to the word. I also have my own experiences to remember when all looked grim, and God used it for my good.

March 12

And we all, who with unveiled faces contemplate the Lord's glory, are being transformed into his image with ever-increasing glory, which comes from the Lord, who is the Spirit.
—2 CORINTHIANS 3:18

Someone told me many years ago, "The closer you get to God, the narrower your road will get."

This is good. It limits the decisions I have to make.

March 13

*Now faith is confidence in what we hope for and
assurance about what we do not see.*
—HEBREWS 11:1

I have seen many miracles in my life. I couldn't stop drinking and drugging. When I surrendered to God, he took care of it. I had to do some work, but he had the ultimate power. The is true for my other addictions. God will do the same for the cancer.

March 14

Let us then approach God's throne of grace with confidence, so that we may receive mercy and find grace to help us in our time of need.
—HEBREWS 4:16

Approaching God's throne with confidence can still be difficult for me. I believe God will help others in their time of need. I still have doubts that he will help me.

When my negative thoughts takeover I look to my experience. This can include repeating over and over again scriptures or prayers, talking with others, journaling, or writing out the problem on a piece of paper and putting it in my God Box. He always comes through in my time of need.

March 15

For our struggle is not against flesh and blood, but against the
rulers, against the authorities, against the powers of this dark world
and against the spiritual forces of evil in the heavenly realms.
—EPHESIANS 6:12

Since I have been diagnosed with cancer I have been on constant vigilance against evil forces. My mind can be my worst enemy.

This is a sample of my thoughts, "My next computerized axial tomography (CAT) scan is going to show the cancer has spread. The doctors say the longest any lives are five years once diagnosed."

I tell myself for every evil force there are just as many heavenly ones. These heavenly forces are there for my good. They give me strength for the battles and the war against evil. They have already won. It is futile for evil to attempt to hit me with poisonous arrows. I have the Healer and Savior surrounding me.

March 16

*So we make it our goal to please him, whether we
are at home in the body or away from it.*
—2 Corinthians 5:9

This is how I lived my life with God. I went back and forth. I never committed. My journey with God didn't have to be as difficult as it was. I made it so by not believing he wanted what was best for me, believing I had to be perfect, and believing he couldn't forgive me for all I had done. I realized none of this was true. He wanted me to grow. I just had to try. My heart had to be in alignment with his, and now it is.

Devote yourselves to prayer, being watchful and thankful.
—Colossians 4:2

How could I be thankful for having cancer? How could I be thankful for being an alcoholic and drug addict?

I have been sober and drug free for over 32 years. I have shared my experience, strength and hope to help others realize it is possible to live life on life's term without drinking or drugging. It also began my journey with the God of my understanding. I learned he loved me, and showered me with grace, mercy, and forgiveness.

I was diagnosed with cancer. It took me a few months to realize how I could use my experience to possibly help others. I began writing this meditation book.

March 18

Blessed are those who have learned to acclaim you,
who walk in the light of your presence, Lord.
—PSALM 89:15

My journey with acclaiming God has been slow. I still struggle with it. I don't have a problem proclaiming God in meetings or with my family and close friends.

I do have a problem in public. When I pull into a public place listening to a spiritual speaker, I turn the volume down. This way the people won't hear what I am listening too. I can't change until I notice a change needs to be made.

I was driving through a construction zone listening to a spiritual speaker. This time I didn't turn the volume down. I noticed, as I was passing by a worker, he was listening too. He nodded at me. I drove on realizing I had made a small positive change.

March 19

As for God, his way is perfect: The Lord's word is flawless; he shields all who take refuge in him.
—2 SAMUEL 22:31

I have to remember that God is perfect, and I am not. It doesn't work when I try to take control. I know this in my head, but I still do it.

I turn it over to God because all else has failed. It is like a weight has been lifted from me. I know that God will protect me and take care of me.

March 20

Two are better than one, because they have a good return for their labor: If either of them falls down, one can help the other up. But pity anyone who falls and has no one to help them up. Also, if two lie down together, they will keep warm. But how can one keep warm alone? Though one may be overpowered, two can defend themselves. A cord of three strands is not quickly broken.
—ECCLESIASTES 4:9-12

I needed other people to show me how to live life without drinking and drugging. I couldn't have done it alone. If God wanted me to do it alone, I would be alone. Thank God I am not.

I have a person I talk with who had lung cancer. She has been cancer-free for eight years. She has been an invaluable asset to me through my tears, questions, and good news. She has walked with me through this journey.

March 21

*for all have sinned and fall short of the glory of
God, and all are justified freely by his grace through
the redemption that came by Christ Jesus.*
—ROMANS 3:23-24

Thank you, God. I know God didn't give up on me. He found a way to redeem me, so I could live with him in this life and the next.

March 22

Do not deceive yourselves. If any of you think you are wise by the standards of this age, you should become fools so that you may become wise. For the wisdom of this world is foolishness in God's sight. As it is written: He catches the wise in their craftiness.
—1 CORINTHIANS 3:18-19

I have tried to be slick and do what I knew in my heart to be wrong. I eventually learned from my own actions the pain I caused not only God and others, but myself as well. God knows what's best for me, and he has all the answers.

March 23

*The secret things belong to the Lord our God, but the
things revealed belong to us and to our children forever,
that we may follow all the words of this law.*
—DEUTERONOMY 29:29

Some situations in my life I won't have the complete answer too. I
believe God knows what is best. This builds my faith in him.

March 24

Love must be sincere. Hate what is evil; cling to what is good. Be devoted to one another in love. Honor one another above yourselves.
—ROMANS 12:9-10

Love means expecting nothing in return. If I give money to someone, I give it without expecting them to return it to me. If I get angry at them, I didn't give the money for the right reason in the first place. This is also the same for emotional support.

March 25

*Because of the Lord's great love we are not
consumed, for his compassions never fail.*
—LAMENTATIONS 3:22

If I got what I deserve, I wouldn't be here. I wouldn't be able to share my experience, strength, and hope living with cancer.

March 26

Moses my servant is dead. Now then, you and all these
people, get ready to cross the Jordan River into the land
I am about to give to them—to the Israelites.
—JOSHUA 1:2

God makes promises to his people. We might not believe him. God
keeps his promises. It doesn't matter how long it takes.

March 27

The Lord makes firm the steps of the one who
delights in him; though he may stumble, he will not
fall, for the Lord upholds him with his hand.
—Psalm 37:23-24

I have fallen, stumbled, tripped, and taken detours. Through it all, God has been holding my hand, lifting me up, and carrying me through this battle with the cancer.

March 28

*Be completely humble and gentle; be patient, bearing
with one another in love. Make every effort to keep the
unity of the Spirit through the bond of peace.*
—EPHESIANS 4:2-3

In my experience I haven't been completely humble, gentle, patient, or peaceful with others, and there have been consequences. It was because of these consequences I continue to learn how to act towards others. It is so much easier when I give up and give it to God.

March 29

Remain in me, as I also remain in you. No branch can bear fruit by itself; it must remain in the vine. Neither can you bear fruit unless you remain in me.
—JOHN 15:4

God is in me. He is healing me from this disease just like he has healed me of other diseases. His spirit flows through me.

I have tried to leave him in the past, and I went my own way. Did it work? Not for me. I will remain. It is much easier.

March 30

Therefore, since we have been justified through faith, we have peace with God through our Lord Jesus Christ, through whom we have gained access by faith into this grace in which we now stand. And we boast in the hope of the glory of God.
—ROMANS 5:1-2

All I have to do is believe. If I have just a little faith, this is all I need to get on the road of recovery. If I take a step towards Him, he beckons me to Him. The closer I move towards him, the easier it gets.

March 31

*Bring joy to your servant, Lord, for I put my trust in you. You,
Lord, are forgiving and good, abounding in love to all who call to you.*
—Psalm 86:4-5

God has been good to me. He has forgiven me of all my sins. The
ones I remember; the ones I don't; and, unfortunately, the ones I have
yet to commit.

The way I lived my life damage has been done to my body. There has
also been harm to my body in which I had no part. Either way, God loves
me the same. He is my Doctor and my Healer.

April 1

And we know that in all things God works for the good of those who love him, who have been called according to his purpose.
—ROMANS 8:28

The cancer has been used for my good. It has enabled me to do with utmost confidence what I have always wanted to do—write. I have become even stronger spiritually.

Isn't this the ultimate goal to have a deeper relationship with God?

April 2

Take delight in the Lord, and he will give
you the desires of your heart.
—Psalm 37:4

I have always known right from wrong. I feel I was inherently born to know the difference. I was fortunate enough to have parents and other role models instill in me the difference.

There were actions I knew deep in my soul that were wrong to myself and others. My basic needs were met, but my spiritual, mental, and emotional ones were dying.

I gave up and turned my will and life over to God. I began to get fed spiritually, mentally, and emotionally. Even though I have the disease of cancer. I continue to be fed, and the desires of my heart continue to be given to me.

April 3

Therefore he is able to save completely those who come to God
through him, because he always lives to intercede for them.
—HEBREWS 7:25

Jesus is my intercessor. If it weren't for him, I wouldn't be sitting here spreading the word of his miraculous healing powers.

April 4

I will give you every place where you set
your foot, as I promised Moses.
—JOSHUA 1:3

God keeps his promises. All he asks is that we trust him and do what he asks. Why? Because he knows what is best for us.

I found out I had cancer. It was hard to trust God, and to believe God knew what was best for me. I have found when I do trust I have a peace beyond explanation.

For God, who said, "Let light shine out of darkness,"
made his light shine in our hearts to give us the light of the
knowledge of God's glory displayed in the face of Christ.
—2 CORINTHIANS 4:6

God is my source. He has the power. If I don't believe this, all I need to do is take one look at my life. God grabbed the reigns and healed me when I surrendered my imagined power. All I had to do was ask.

April 6

*With great power the apostles continued to testify to the
resurrection of the Lord Jesus. And God's grace was so
powerfully at work in them all that there were no needy persons
among them. For from time to time those who owned land
or houses sold them, brought the money from the sales.*
—ACTS 4:33-34

God's grace is unending. In spite of my thoughts and actions God has given me undeserved favor. I believe he put me with people who have the same beliefs.

I need others. If God wanted me to do it alone, there wouldn't be other people on earth. We help each other out spiritually, physically, or materially.

April 7

I will repay you for the years the locusts have eaten—the
great locust and the young locust, the other locusts and the
locust swarm—my great army that I sent among you.
—JOEL 2:25

After I turned my life over to God, I knew I wouldn't go hungry. I would always be taking care of in all areas of my life.

April 8

The good man out of the good treasure of his heart brings forth what is good; and the evil man out of the evil treasure brings forth what is evil; for his mouth speaks from that which fills his heart.
—LUKE 6:45

My life is much more peaceful and joyful when I am kind to others. If, I sow good then I receive good, which creates a domino effect.

The good will smother the evil. I breathe in life and healing and breathe out fear and disease every day. I am being healed.

April 9

They did not dislodge the Canaanites living in Gezer;
to this day the Canaanites live among the people of
Ephraim but are required to do forced labor.
—JOSHUA 16:10

I know what God wants me to do and how to live. There are always consequences when I don't. God knows what is best for me. I have realized he will have his way, either sooner or later.

April 10

Therefore we do not lose heart. Though outwardly we are
wasting away, yet inwardly we are being renewed day by day.
—2 CORINTHIANS 4:16

We all have to perish, but it's just our body. I am renewed each and every day. I am being healed from cancer as I write this. When I do perish in this life I will be completely renewed.

April 11

*Let us acknowledge the Lord; let us press on to acknowledge
him. As surely as the sun rises, he will appear; he will come to us
like the winter rains, like the spring rains that water the earth.*
—HOSEA 6:3

God quenches my thirst for him. He feeds my soul. He is healing me.

April 12

*For Christ's love compels us, because we are convinced
that one died for all, and therefore all died.*
—2 CORINTHIANS 5:14

I was always trying to succeed in life. Success meant to me how much money I made; where I lived; or how many people liked me.

My goal is to be on equal grounds with everyone. The person—who lives in a tent, in a house, or on the street—is the same inside as the person living in a penthouse. We all have the same fears and feelings. My life got so much easier when I realized this.

April 13

*I have spoken to you with great frankness; I take great pride in you.
I am greatly encouraged; in all our troubles my joy knows no bounds.*
—2 CORINTHIANS 7:4

I have to give all credit to God. For the peace I have in my life despite my circumstances, and for anything good in my life.

April 14

Remember the command that Moses the servant
of the Lord gave you after he said, "The Lord your
God will give you rest by giving you this land."
—JOSHUA 1:13

I compare this verse in relation to my children. They know I have their best interest at heart, but they still do things I don't like or approve. This doesn't mean I am going to change my plans for them, which are for their good, comfort, and peace.

April 15

And pray in the Spirit on all occasions with all kinds of prayers and requests. With this in mind, be alert and always keep on praying for all the Lord's people.
—EPHESIANS 6:18

I have to constantly be on guard against the negative voices in my head. They want me dead either physically, mentally, or spiritually. If I listen to the voices long enough, they will begin to bring me down, and it's a downhill spiral from there. I sometimes can see it happening, and I wallow in it.

I don't do this as long. It's not pleasant, and I have had enough of the internal peace and serenity that I want it. I had lived in the negative for so long. It was the only life I knew. It took practice, practice, and more practice; perseverance; and a willingness to believe in God for my life to slowly take a change for the better.

April 16

And whatsoever ye do in word or deed, do all in the name of
the Lord Jesus, giving thanks to God and the Father by him.
—Colossians 3:17

I have lived in self-will only thinking of myself. I know the only reason I am here is because of God. I am here to help others with strengthening their belief.

April 17

Finally, be strong in the Lord and in his mighty power.
—Ephesians 6:10

God is my strength. He gives me the power to live day to day with this disease that wants me dead, and to enjoy each moment, no matter what the circumstances.

April 18

For it is by grace you have been saved, through faith—
and this is not from yourselves, it is the gift of God.
—EPHESIANS 2:8

All I have to do is believe that God's grace will save me and heal me from all diseases.

April 19

"He answered, "Love the Lord your God with all your heart and with all your soul and with all your strength and with all your mind; and, Love your neighbor as yourself."
—Luke 10:27

When I love the Lord my God with all my heart, all my soul, all my strength, and all my mind I can't help but to love myself and others. I love myself enough today to take breaks; to take care of myself; to do what the doctor says; and to treat others as I want to be treated. Some days are better than others.

April 20

The Lord will march out like a champion, like a warrior
he will stir up his zeal; with a shout he will raise the
battle cry and will triumph over his enemies.
—Isaiah 42:13

The Lord is my warrior. He fights for me when I don't have the strength that day or moment to fight for myself. I know he is always there for me even when I feel alone. He surrounds me with his presence.

April 21

Out of his fullness we have all received grace
in place of grace already given.
—JOHN 1:16

God is there with his grace waiting for me to ask for it. His grace is for everyone. I considered myself beyond redeemable. Once I asked grace was given, and I became part of his family. His grace heals me.

April 22

in whom are hidden all the treasures of wisdom and knowledge. I tell you this so that no one may deceive you by fine-sounding arguments.
—COLOSSIANS 2:3-4

I made a commitment to serve God when I surrendered my will and life over to him. This is part of serving God to write of how his power entered into my life, and I began to heal and live.

April 23

I wish that all of you were as I am. But each of you has your own gift from God; one has this gift, another has that.
—1 CORINTHIANS 7:7

I remember writing poems in grade school. I loved reading and researching. When I got out of high school I began working in a Public Affairs Office. I decided to get a degree in journalism. I continued to write poems, news releases, speeches, and radio spots.

I started many books, but I never finished. I then was diagnosed with cancer. I had always read meditation books and journaled every morning. God made me see that there wasn't really a meditation book for people with cancer. I then knew this is what God wanted me to do.

April 24

He who did not spare his own Son, but gave him up for us all—
how will he not also, along with him, graciously give us all things?
—ROMANS 8:32

He wants me to live for his glory. This is what I am doing. I am giving the glory to him. It's only because of him that I am able to write this book.

April 25

If anyone speaks, they should do so as one who speaks the very words of God. If anyone serves, they should do so with the strength God provides, so that in all things God may be praised through Jesus Christ. To him be the glory and the power for ever and ever. Amen.
—1 PETER 4:11

When I went back for my follow up appointment with the surgeon who had removed my malignant lymph nodes he said, "I don't believe how happy you are. Most people in your position would have given up, sat down, and began watching TV."

I replied, "It is because of God, and the support that I have that I don't."

April 26

*The thief comes only to steal and kill and destroy; I have
come that they may have life, and have to the full.*
—John 10:10

I have been visited by the thief many times. The thief did everything
to destroy me. I knew the only one who could win, not only the battle,
but the war was God.

April 27

Hear my cry for mercy as I call to you for help, as I lift up my hands toward your Most Holy Place.
—PSALM 28:2

My God had every reason to have no mercy for me. I am not saying I didn't have consequences as a result of my actions or non-actions. I called to God, and he was merciful to me. He knew my heart.

April 28

"Come, follow me," Jesus said, "and I will
send you out to fish for people."
—Matthew 4:19

God saved me, and I had a commitment to tell others how God helped me. This commitment wasn't forced. It was to save my life. I am willing and want to serve God.

For the word of God is alive and active. Sharper than any double-edged sword, it penetrates even to dividing soul and spirit, joints and marrow; it judges the thoughts and attitudes of the heart.
—HEBREWS 4:12

God knows every intricate detail of me. He knows I want to obey and spread his message.

April 30

Now to each one the manifestation of the
Spirit is given for the common good.
—1 CORINTHIANS 12:7

God gave me the gift of writing to share my experience, strength, and hope of how he has and continues to work in my life.

May 1

Your beauty should not come from outward adornment, such as elaborate hairstyles and the wearing of gold jewelry or fine clothes. Rather, it should be that of your inner self, the unfading beauty of a gentle and quiet spirit, which is of great worth in God's sight.
—1 PETER 3:3-4

I used to worry about how I looked, the lines on my face, the gray hair, and my body not having its youthful look. I look at myself now after having gone through radiation, chemotherapy, immunotherapy, and many surgeries. Before I thought about my appearance 90% of the time, and now it's down to 20% of the time.

In the end it's not going to matter what I look like. What is going to matter is my relationship with God. I am at more peace now than I have ever been. The world has taken on a different meaning along with my appearance.

May 2

And I heard a loud voice from the throne saying, "Look!
God's dwelling place is now among the people, and
he will dwell with them. They will be his people, and
God himself will be with them and be their God."
—REVELATIONS 21:3

God is with me always. Sometimes I feel it, while at other times I don't. I have experienced and seen God's presence through others' actions. He has sent angels to me for protection and guidance. He sent Jesus to show how much he loves me. One day I will always be in his presence.

May 3

That at the name of Jesus every knee should bow, in heaven and on earth and under the earth, and every tongue acknowledge that Jesus Christ is Lord, to the glory of God the Father.
—PHILIPPIANS 2:10-11

God is my only source. He is my King, my Healer, my employer, and my very life. He works through others, but he is the source. He provides the healing powers.

May 4

For who is God besides the Lord? And who is the Rock except our God? It is God who arms me with strength and keeps my way secure. He makes my feet like the feet of a deer; he causes me to stand on the heights.
—2 SAMUEL 22:32-34

God has seen me through many dilemmas. Through it all he has been my Rock—unmoving, strong, resilient, and giving me strength to go through anything.

May 5

*But the Advocate, the Holy Spirit, whom the Father
will send in my name, will teach you all things and will
remind you of everything I have said to you.*
—JOHN 14:26

I seem to forget the Word when I perceive an event in my life as negative, such as the death of a loved one, financial difficulties, divorce, or a cancer diagnosis. It could also be a happy event—but still life changing—such as the birth of a child, a marriage, or a raise at work. These events cause my relationship with God to deepen.

May 6

*Those who know your name trust in you: for you,
Lord, have never forsaken those who seek you.*
—Psalm 9:10

I was diagnosed with cancer, and I had many different thoughts, questions, and feelings running through my mind, "God has this. What am I going to do? How am I going to tell my mom, brother, and children? I am going to die. I deserve it for all I have done in my past, and how I abused my body. Where is God?"

After my mind quieted down. I did feel forsaken, but my head knew I wasn't. This is where I can do all I can do. The doctors can do all they can do. God has the final word. All I need to do is trust.

May 7

Therefore let all Israel be assured of this: God has made this Jesus, whom you crucified, both Lord and Messiah.
—ACTS 2:36

God saved me in spite of my actions and in-actions. He sent me Jesus to save us. This is how much he loves us.

May 8

To the angel of the church in Philadelphia write: These are the words of him who is holy and true, who holds the key of David. What he opens no one can shut, and what he shuts no one can open.
—REVELATIONS 3:7

Even though my strength weakens day to day I know I will be entering through the door no one can lock. I won't be the one who tries to open the door, which is locked.

But you, Lord, are a shield around me, my
glory, the One who lifts my head high.
—PSALM 3:3

I know God has his shield surrounding me and protecting me from cancer and the treatments. He also protects me from the negative thoughts racing through my head. He has lifted me above the disease and has given me a respite.

May 10

Jesus said to him, "Away from me, Satan! For it is written:
Worship the Lord your God, and serve him only."
—MATTHEW 4:10

Satan tries on a daily basis to get me sidetracked. How does he do this? His latest tool pertains to my disease. Doubting I will get better; thinking I am getting worse; wondering why me; and seeing everyone else living their life.

I have to dig my feet in and know God hasn't abandoned me. I do this by praying; talking with others; and writing what I am grateful for.

May 11

As water reflects the face, so one's life reflects the heart.
—PROVERBS 27:19

Unfortunately, my life has reflected my heart over the years. My life looked like a Dr. Jekyll and Mr. Hyde. I was successful on the outside, but on the inside my life was a total mess. I was a drunk and drug addict.

I turned my will and life over to the care of God. My life began a slow 360 degree turn towards God. My heart began coming into alignment with God.

May 12

*Hear my cry, O God; listen to my prayer. From the ends
of the earth I call to you, I call as my heart grows faint;
lead me to the rock that is higher than I. For you have
been my refuge, a strong tower against the foe.*
—PSALM 61:1-3

There are times when God seems farther away than other times. I have to keep doing what I have always done while I am walking through it—praying, journaling, and meditating. I write my worries on a piece of paper and put them in my God box. This literally lets me visualize giving my worries to God. I write a gratitude list. I help others to get out of my own head.

My experience has shown me this will pass. It is a feeling. God is my refuge.

May 13

*I eagerly expect and hope that I will in no way be ashamed,
but will have sufficient courage so that now as always Christ
will be exalted in my body, whether by life or by death.*
—Philippians 1:20

I was full of shame and guilt before I got sober. I believe these feelings did have a purpose. I don't know if I would have ever made a decision to give God my life until I realized I couldn't stop.

I thought it was the worst day of my life. It ended up being one of the best. This was when I began changing into the person I was meant to be.

I hit another bottom with cancer. I realized I am here only because of God. He has given me an opportunity to experience life on a deeper level and to trust he has this.

May 14

*Just as people are destined to die once,
and after that to face judgment.*
—Hebrews 9:27

My faith has always grown the most after I have gone through a difficult time. I see how God was there all along directing my steps. He kept things away from me that weren't good for me.

I have faced judgment in this life from others and myself. I believe my spirit is letting me know what I have done or am about to do is harmful. Judgment is for my good and nothing can change until I am aware. Just as positive acts have a domino effect so do negative ones.

May 15

Therefore do not be foolish, but understand what the Lord's will is.
—EPHESIANS 5:17

For many years I lived without thinking of consequences. As a result, I suffered much guilt, shame, and humiliation. When I tried to run my life all I did was make a huge mess of it.

I turned my life over to God. My life slowly began getting better. I learned of his grace, mercy, and unending love.

Now if we are children, then we are heirs-heirs of God, and co-heirs with Christ, if indeed we share in his sufferings in order that we may also share in his glory.
—ROMANS 8:17

God, Jesus Christ, and the Holy Spirit, walk side by side with me through this journey called life. If it weren't for this, my days, hours, and minutes living with cancer would be much more difficult to walk through. God provides me with everything I need.

May 17

Now this is eternal life: that they know you, the only true God, and Jesus Christ, whom you have sent.
—JOHN 17:3

Thank God for Jesus for without him I would be doomed. I would have no hope in this life or the next. Life wouldn't have any meaning or purpose. I would be living for myself and not really thinking of others.

May 18

All of them were filled with the Holy Spirit and began to speak in other tongues as the Spirit enabled them.
—ACTS 2:4

I can remember being filled with the Holy Spirit. Something had changed to the inner being of my core. The people around me were skeptical at first. They really didn't believe my words.

They didn't understand the change in me. I found people who spoke my language. They understood what I was saying. Slowly, the others knew I had changed.

May 19

But thanks be to God! He gives us the victory
through our Lord Jesus Christ.
—1 CORINTHIANS 15:57

Jesus is my Savior and Healer. All I have to do is ask in Jesus' name for God to heal me. It will be done even if my faith is only as big as a mustard seed.

May 20

But whoever disowns before others, I will
disown before my Father in heaven.
—MATTHEW 10:33

I always had an internal belief there was a God. There were times in my life when I wouldn't talk about what God had or was doing for me. It was much easier to talk in Alcoholics Anonymous (AA) or Al-Anon meetings about Him.

In public, it was a whole different story. One wouldn't think I had a relationship with God. I was a slow learner. All one had to do was watch me in a grocery story line, huffing and puffing, when I thought the line was moving too slow

Today, I am much better in public only because of God. I talk more about God, but I still need much improvement in this area.

May 21

But very truly I tell you, it is for your good that I am going away. Unless I go away, the Advocate will not come to you; but if I go, I will send him to you.
—John 16:7

The Advocate or Holy Spirit guides me and directs me. He is on my side. He wants what is best for me. There are many times what is best for me will help others. My Holy Spirit has directed me to write this meditation book for him, others, and even myself.

May 22

*Who is wise? Let them realize these things. Who is discerning?
Let them understand. The ways of the Lord are right; the
righteous walk in them, but the rebellious stumble in them.*
—HOSEA 14:9

It took me many years to learn that the Lord's ways were the easiest. I stumbled and fell many times. I tried my way over and over again until it didn't work.

I observed the people, who had God in their life and were living according to his instructions. They had a more peaceful, serene, and easier life. I trust the Lord who is walking with me through this new trial in my life.

May 23

About three in the afternoon Jesus cried out in a loud voice, "Eli, Eli, lema sabachthani? (which means My God, my God, why have you forsaken me?)"
—MATTHEW 27:46

Even Jesus was not exempt from human feelings. He knew fear. He knew anger. He knew love. He knew us. He knew what he had to do. He was still afraid.

Do I like having cancer? No, but it will be for the ultimate good.

May 24

Each one should test their own actions. Then they can take pride in themselves alone, without comparing themselves to someone else.
—GALATIANS 6:4

I have bragged or secretly been smug about my accomplishments. Eventually, I will compare myself to others, and I won't measure up. This isn't a way to live. It doesn't bring much peace.

Today, I know my achievements are only from God. I am his vessel. Even when times are tough my life is ultimately used for his purpose.

~ 145 ~

May 25

Therefore, if anyone is in Christ, the new creation
has come: The old has gone, the new is here!
—2 CORINTHIANS 5:17

The way I was living wasn't working, and I had to let God have my life. He was the only one who could change me. I was convicted, miserable, ashamed, and full of all kinds of negative feelings. When I repented my life began to change.

I began to live for God. I am not saying I didn't make many mistakes along the way. I faced many trials and tribulations due to my own actions or nonactions.

The cancer I am living with is in God's hands. I know this. God is using this for his purpose. He is showing his Power.

May 26

So what shall I do? I will pray with my spirit, but I will also pray with my understanding; I will sing with my spirit, but I will also sing with my understanding.
—1 CORINTHIANS 14:15

My understanding has changed over the years. My spirit knows what is best for me. I feel sometimes my spirit prays for me when I don't even know what to pray for. I trust that my spirit knows how to communicate on my behalf.

May 27

But seek first his kingdom and his righteousness;
and all these things will be given to you as well.
—MATTHEW 6:33

By the time I found out I had cancer, I thought I had a good relationship with God. I realized as I told my friends, "I guess God wanted more of my attention."

I changed little things making a big difference in my cancer recovery. Whenever I got in my car I began listening to spiritual podcasts. In my morning meditations I wrote down anything that would help me with my attitude and outlook on life. I began watching positive or funny programs. Doing these little actions made a big difference.

May 28

Meanwhile we groan, longing to be clothed
instead with our heavenly dwelling.
—2 CORINTHIANS 5:2

I am not above it all. I have learned that God is above it all. He is going to take care of all diseases, enemies, or actions that were meant for my harm.

May 29

The one who does what is sinful is of the devil, because the devil has been sinning from the beginning. The reason the Son of God appeared was to destroy the devil's work.
—1 JOHN 3:8

I am grateful for the Son of God. My experience has shown me my past was a miserable way to live. I believe my road has gotten narrower. Jesus has a way of removing my sins when I give up, sometimes immediately and at other times over time. Either way it is always best for me.

May 30

We all, like sheep, have gone astray, each of us has turned to our
own way; and the Lord has laid on him the iniquity of us all.
—Isaiah 53:6

He definitely is my Savior. Without him I would be lost, and full of fear, especially living with the disease of cancer. God is healing me. It's never too late to ask for help.

May 31

*Put on the full armor of God, so that you can take
your stand against the devil's schemes.*
—EPHESIANS 6:11

Satan is sneaky. He weasels his way into my mind telling me all kinds of lies. I drank alcohol, did all kinds of drugs, and smoked cigarettes. I thought I had to have these things to get through life.

God in his grace and mercy made me realize these things didn't work any longer. He gave me the strength to stop by putting on his full armor. He is eradicating the cancer in the same manner.

June 1

He guides the humble in what is right and teaches them his way.
—PSALM 25:9

Once I realized God was the answer it was much easier for me to seek his way. I humbly offered myself to him, so he could show me his direction and guidance.

As a result, my life has been much easier and peaceful.

June 2

*and if you spend yourselves in behalf of the hungry and satisfy
the needs of the oppressed, then your light will rise in the
darkness, and your night will become like the noonday.*
—ISAIAH 58:10

Nothing can compare to a grateful spirit. I can feel the spirit running through me. It is a gentle, understanding, and compassionate spirit.

The first time I met my oncologist I felt immediately at ease. He calmed my spirit down just by his presence. The nurses, radiologist oncologists, brain surgeons, and others displayed the same characteristics. God lined up the right people in my life to do battle with the cancer.

June 3

On one occasion, while he was eating with them, he gave them this command: "Do not leave Jerusalem, but wait for the gift my Father promised, which you have heard me speak about. For John baptized with water, but in a few days you will be baptized with the Holy Spirit."
—ACTS 1:4-5

I went to my primary care physician for almost a year with hip pain. I would feel better for a few days. I was beginning to feel like a hypochondriac. A little voice kept telling me to ask him to order a CAT scan of my lungs.

Months before I had one done. It showed nodes that could turn cancerous. The report said I should have one done every six to nine months. I thought he would have ordered one, if he felt I needed it.

The pain kept getting worse, and it had become almost unbearable. The voice was getting louder and louder. I asked him to order a CAT scan.

He began to disagree with me. I explained to him about the previous one, and it was past the time frame to have one done. He looked back in my chart and saw I did need one. He ordered it, and I found out I had lung cancer, which had spread to my hip.

June 4

*May he give you the desire of your heart and make
all your plans succeed. May we shout for joy over
your victory and lift up our banners in the name of
our God. May the Lord grant all your requests.*
—Psalm 20:4-5

I was in the grocery store with my two small children. One was trying to crawl out of the cart. My other was at the bottom making animal noises. I was asking myself, "Are my kids going to be all right?"

This older woman with the brightest, prettiest, and hypnotizing blue eyes and white hair appeared out of nowhere. She was so quiet it made me jump.

She looked me straight in my eyes and said, "Your girls are going to be all right. They're going to grow up and be fine."

I can't even remember what I said. I was in shock. It did calm me down. Whenever I felt over whelmed she would pop into my head. It dawned on me this had been a message from God sent through an angel.

My children have grown into fine young ladies.

June 5

*Therefore you do not lack any spiritual gift as you
eagerly wait for our Lord Jesus Christ to be revealed.
He will also keep you firm to the end, so that you will
be blameless on the day of our Lord Jesus Christ.*
—1 CORINTHIANS 1:7-8

How true. Thank God I know this in my head and finally in my soul.

June 6

Walk in obedience to all that the Lord your God has commanded you, so that you may live and prosper and prolong your days in the land that you will possess.
—Deuteronomy 5:33

God got my attention when it was confirmed I had cancer. I was so scared, sad, and full of emotions. I didn't want to feel. God was the only one who could walk with me through this process, and the people he chose to put in my life.

My walk with him has become more focused, and my ways have become more like his ways. He has prolonged my life longer than I deserve.

June 7

When he had received the drink, Jesus said, "It is finished."
With that, he bowed his head and gave up his spirit.
—1 JOHN 19:30

With the torturous death of Jesus, my life was eternally saved. Do I escape pain or even death? No. Even Jesus didn't escape death.

In this life we lose people we hold dear, and there is pain and grief. After going through this dark tunnel, we realize there was something at the end for our good.

June 8

*Who can live and not see death, or who can
escape the power of the grave?*
—PSALM 89:48

No one can escape death. Jesus didn't even escape death. He knew the outcome, but he still experienced apprehension and dread.

We realize how really powerless we are. We aren't in control and never were. We are here for God and others. Our life can be much easier with God or more difficult without him.

June 9

As no one has power over the wind to contain it, so no one has power over the time of their death. As no one is discharged in time of war, so wickedness will not release those who practice it.
—ECCLESIATES 8:8

It's true. I don't know when I will die. Only God knows. I have experienced many deaths in my life. The dependence upon drugs, alcohol, and cigarettes. My children going to kindergarten. My children growing up. The death of loved ones. Friends moving on. These experiences have shown me I will live forever in the next realm, and God is not finished with me yet.

June 10

I can do all this through him who gives me strength.
—PHILIPPIANS 4:13

Living with the diagnosis and treatment of cancer has shown me it is only Christ who has given me the strength to live each day in relative peace and happiness.

June 11

*By wisdom a house is built, and through understanding
it is established; through knowledge its rooms are
filled with rare and beautiful treasures.*
—PROVERBS 24:3-4

A house to me is the body in which my soul lives. I have more wisdom and grown over the years from many mistakes and from taking correct and incorrect actions.

The diagnosis of cancer was good for me because I then understood the brevity of life. It made me become knowledgeable of what was important in life—do unto others and treat others as I want to be treated.

June 12

Jesus answered, "It is written: Man shall not live on bread alone, but on every word that comes from the mouth of God."
—Matthew 4:1

I need food to eat and the word to live. I could have given up and lived a miserable and depressing life. I am not implying I don't experience the feelings of fear, depression, or anxiety. I do, but it doesn't last as long.

June 13

I am the living bread which came down from heaven.
Whoever eats this bread will live forever. This bread is
my flesh, which I will give for the life of the world.
—John 6:51

I have to eat for nourishment and drink for survival. The better I take care of myself. The better I function or live in this life.

Jesus is telling me I need his food and drink to survive in the spiritual world, as well as this world. I don't do this just once. I have to eat and drink the Word every day.

June 14

Consider it pure joy, my brothers and sisters, whenever
you face trials of many kinds, because you know that
the testing of your faith produces perseverance.
—JAMES 1:2-3

God has taught me many lessons in perseverance. The first seemed daunting and overwhelming. Through each experience my faith and trust in God grew.

Living with the disease of cancer is another trial I am experiencing. I know deep in my being God is with me and for me. Jesus is speaking on my behalf, and the Holy Spirit is guiding me through this experience. I am grateful to have the Trinity with and through me.

June 15

But I have prayed for you, Simon, that your faith may not fail.
And when you have turned back, strengthen your brothers.
—LUKE 22:32

Jesus knows what is coming. My faith has been tested. When I stood strong it showed others how God turns what was meant for my downfall to be for my good.

June 16

Peter replied, "Repent and be baptized, every one of you,
in the name of Jesus Christ for the forgiveness of your
sins. And you will receive the gift of the Holy Spirit."
—Acts 2:38

I remember when I was baptized. I was trying to stop drinking, drugging, and living a life I was ashamed of. I remember thinking it didn't take because I still drank.

Two weeks later, God led me to a group of people who had stopped drinking and drugging. This was when my spiritual journey began. I needed the two weeks to totally surrender to God.

June 17

Then Jesus told them, "This very night you will all fall away on account of me, for it is written: 'I will strike the shepherd, and the sheep of the flock will be scattered.'"
—MATTHEW 26:31

How many times have I kept my mouth shut about the power of God, and what he has done for me? I don't have a problem among others who are like-minded. I still do when I am around others I don't know.

I went to my oncologist, and, overall, it was a good report. I told him it must have been the meditating I had been doing. I meant it, but I left out about my praying, journaling, and reading scriptures. This was all implied. I still need improvement in this area.

June 18

*Taste and see that the Lord is good; blessed is the one
who takes refuge in him. Fear the Lord, you his holy
people, for those who fear him lack nothing.*
—PSALM 34:8-9

When I seek his wisdom, his word, and his ways I have had all I need, and even more than I deserve.

June 19

I will remain in the world no longer, but they are still
in the world, and I am coming to you. Holy Father,
protect them by the power of your name, the name you
gave me, so that they may be one as we are one.
—JOHN 17:11

Jesus continues to pray, ask, and intercede to his Father for us. He has never stopped.

*Therefore, since we are surrounded by such a great cloud
of witnesses, let us throw off everything that hinders
and the sin that so easily entangles. And let us run
with perseverance the race marked out for us.*
—HEBREWS 12:1

There is always someone out there to help me through all my issues, whether here on earth or in the heavenly realm. My race is sometimes hard and at other times restful, but it requires a lot of practice.

June 21

Be kind and compassionate to one another, forgiving each other, just as in Christ God forgave you.
—EPHESIANS 4:32

I can hear my mom saying, "You'll get more with sugar than vinegar."

My dad used to tell me, "Watch how you treat people on the way up because on the way back down some of them you'll meet along the way."

I am the last person who can judge anyone with my past. Do I still do it? Yes, not as bad as I used too.

I have learned. The easier I am on others. The easier I am on myself.

June 22

Who through faith are shielded by God's power until the coming of the salvation that is ready to be revealed in the last time.
—1 PETER 1:5

I have come to believe God is my source. He has the power. It is healing and lifesaving. It can destroy or divert persons, spirits, or demons intended for my harm.

June 23

See to it that no one falls short of the grace of God and that
no bitter root grows up to cause trouble and defile many.
—HEBREWS 12:15

I am harming myself when harboring a resentment. Somehow this seeps out contaminating and infecting others in a harmful way. It is best for me to pull up the resentment root and all.

June 24

Truly my soul finds rest in God; my salvation comes
from him. Truly he is my rock and my salvation;
he is my fortress, I will never be shaken.
—PSALM 62:1-2

My soul can't find the ultimate rest, comfort, and protection from other people, places, or things. My solid foundation is from the Lord. People, places, and things can fail me. God is always there waiting to comfort and protect me.

June 25

Do not be carried away by all kinds of strange teachings. It is good for our hearts to be strengthened by grace, not by eating ceremonial foods, which is of no benefit to those who do so.
—HEBREWS 13:9

It is good to eat healthy food for our bodies. In the end it is what is in our spiritual hearts that matter. God's grace is what will carry me through the disease of cancer, the disease of others, and the disease of this world.

June 26

Jesus turned and said to Peter, "Get behind me, Satan!
You are a stumbling block to me; you do not have in mind
the concerns of God, but merely human concerns."
—Matthew 16:23

When I am thinking of what others have done to me, or what they aren't doing for me. When I want more material things. Where is God in all this?

Satan tries his best to corrupt my thinking, which affects my living. He is very sneaky. I have to be on constant guard from the one who wants to destroy me.

God's way is a more peaceful and sane way of living.

June 27

*The Son is the radiance of God's glory and the exact
representation of his being, sustaining all things by his
powerful word. After he had provided purification for sins,
he sat down at the right hand of the Majesty in heaven.*
—HEBREWS 1:3

Jesus shows me God is very forgiving, merciful, and graceful. I think of the woman by the well. Some of the world would still condemn her.

I know others have judged me for my past and present. Some of the world would think I deserve the cancer I have. God's grace, mercy, and forgiveness uses it to show his mighty power.

June 28

For God so loved the world that he gave his one and only Son,
that whoever believes in him shall not perish but have eternal life.
—JOHN 3:16

God loves me. He sent his Son so we would be forgiven. He has given me a second chance at life.

We all have to live before we die. How am I going to live today? Am I going to be depressed, in self-pity, or woe is me because I have cancer? Or am I going to enjoy the beauty of this world God created for me?

June 29

*And God placed all things under his feet and appointed
him to be head over everything for the church.*
—EPHESIANS 1:22

When I was running the show, or God was letting me run the show.
I realized what a total disaster I made of my life. I turned to him in utter
despair.

I haven't regretted turning my life over to God. It has been much
easier to live life with God at the center: spiritually, mentally, emotionally,
and physically.

June 30

*For the bread of God is the bread that comes down
from heaven and gives life to the world.*
—JOHN 6:33

God gives me living bread. He takes care of all my needs. He shows me his power, grace, mercy, forgiveness, and his indescribable love for me.

July 1

Jesus answered, "I am the way and the truth and the life.
No one comes to the Father except through me."
—JOHN 14:6

I am eternally grateful Jesus saved my soul, spirit, and life. He is my Intercessor. He pleads my case. He is my Advocate. He has my best interest at heart.

July 2

In him and through faith in him we may approach
God with freedom and confidence.
—EPHESIANS 3:12

All I have to do is ask in Jesus' name. He takes the reigns and heads straight to God. It might be an answer I don't understand, but the answer is for my ultimate good.

July 3

*For Christ also suffered once for sins, the righteous for
the unrighteous, to bring you to God. He was put to
death in the body but made alive in the Spirit.*
—1 PETER 3:18

God provided a final answer to a dilemma. It has been finished.

July 4

The angel said to the women, "Do not be afraid, for I know that you are looking for Jesus, who was crucified. He is not here; he has risen, just as he said. Come and see the place where he lay."
—MATTHEW 28:5-6

This message was given to anyone who has been judged and persecuted and has harshly judged themselves. This message brings me hope because Jesus gave it to people like me.

July 5

If I rise on the wings of the dawn, if I settle on the far side of the sea,
even there your hand will guide me, your right hand will hold me fast.
—PSALM 139:9-10

God is always with me even when I can't feel, see, or touch him through others. Even when I feel alone because of the cancer God is leading me to recovery and holding my right hand. The hand signifying strength and power.

July 6

Dear friends, since God so loved us, we
also ought to love one another.
—1 John 4:11

I was angry with my primary care physician when I was diagnosed with cancer. I had gone to his office for over a year. I finally demanded a CAT scan of my chest. I had lung cancer, which had spread to my hip and femur.

I bad-mouthed him whenever I had the chance. I didn't say his name, if people were listening, they could figure out who he was. I was going to sue him and talked with three different attorneys.

I discussed my behavior with someone, whom I considered my spiritual advisor. I might have been right, but it didn't give me the right to assassinate his character. He was a human being doing the best he could with the information he had. I realized, if I had gotten what I deserved, I wouldn't be writing this. Therefore, he deserved the same mercy, grace, and forgiveness from me.

July 7

Commit your way to the Lord; trust in him and he will do this.
—Psalm 37:5

Thank God my hip began to hurt. It wasn't getting better with physical therapy, massages, stretching, yoga, exercise, or the chiropractor. It kept getting worse. This prompted me to ask for the CAT scan. God takes care of me.

July 8

Now give me this hill country that the Lord promised me that day. You yourself heard then that the Anakites were there and their cities were large and fortified, but, the Lord helping me, I will drive them out just as he said.
—JOSHUA 14:12

When God is on my side no one or nothing can defeat me. Cancer can't stand against the power of God. He can smite it out of my body.

And he said: "Truly I tell you, unless you change and become like little children, you will never enter the kingdom of heaven."
—MATTHEW 18:3

As a l child I believed anything my dad and mom told me. I wasn't going hungry. I had a place to live. I was loved. The world was a place to be explored. One person, whom I trusted, was controlled by his own disease. His disease not only affected me, but others in my family.

I began to live my life in survival mode, and I was definitely angry at God. My life was great as long as everything was going my way. It wasn't a fun way to live.

I realized what the person did to me wasn't him. It was his disease. It was Satan, and I was letting this affect every area of my life. Satan had accomplished his goal. He had pulled me away from God.

I ran back to God like a lost child. He was always there waiting for me, so he could love and take care of me.

July 10

And lead us not into temptation, but deliver us from the evil one.
—MATTHEW 6:13

I believe evil can include our thinking. I was diagnosed with cancer. I had the opportunity to practice diverting my thinking. I am not implying or saying I don't still have negative thoughts come into my head. It takes practice, practice, practice, and more practice to divert my negative thoughts.

What do I do? I inundate myself with spiritual messages. I talk with others who are uplifting. I feel my feelings. I don't live in denial. I am proactive with my disease. I ask questions. I quote scripture. I watch funny programs. I listen to music. I help others. I journal.

July 11

*Praise be to the God and Father of our Lord Jesus
Christ, who has blessed us in the heavenly realms
with every spiritual blessing in Christ.*
—EPHESIANS 1:3

I am God's child. At times my life doesn't seem to be. My experience has revealed to me over and over again I am God's child. I felt cursed when I was diagnosed with cancer. Over a year-and-a-half later, I know I am blessed.

July 12

You, dear children, are from God and have overcome them, because the one who is in you is greater than the one who is in the world.
—1 JOHN 4:4

There are days when life happens, and I get upset. What do I do? I grumble, complain, and feel sorry for myself. Sometimes I think, "to top it all off I have cancer."

Sometimes, I begin spelling the Serenity Prayer. Other times, I say out loud, "In the name of Jesus Christ, Satan get behind me."

One time I was getting all worked up while I was trying to work on the house. I said out loud, "You can burn the house down, but God is with me. I will still be alright."

These actions made calmer, and I went on with the rest of my day.

July 13

Yet to all who did receive him, to those who believed in his name, he gave the right to become children of God.
—JOHN 1:12

What does it mean to become a child of God?

I have the ultimate assurance someone is always rooting for me. He is my father. He is always on my side. I am more confident. God's values are important to me.

What is your definition?

Blind Pharisee! First clean the inside of the cup and dish, and then the outside also will be clean.
—MATTHEW 23:26

The inside is what matters because it reflects the outside.

I compare it to a person who loses a lot of weight and keeps it off. The person goes out and buys new clothes. The person's outward appearance changed completely because the person underwent an internal transformation.

July 15

*To them God has chosen to make known among
the Gentiles the glorious riches of this mystery,
which is Christ in you, the hope of glory.*
—COLOSSIANS 1:27

God is all inclusive. There aren't any outsiders. No one has done too much evil who isn't welcome. There isn't anyone who is black-balled.

Praise God.

July 16

*Brothers and sisters, I do not consider myself yet to
have taken hold of it. But one thing I do: Forgetting
what is behind and straining toward what is ahead.*
—PHILIPPIANS 3:13

The past can be a great tool to learn about myself. My problem? I have a tendency to stare, wallow, or get lost in it. If I live in the past, I am not living in the day. I am not optimistic about the future.

The past has taught me to be more understanding and less judgmental of others; to listen to my head and not my emotions; to listen to others and not planning my response; and to stay in the day.

If we claim to be without sin, we deceive ourselves and the truth is not in us. If we confess our sins, he is faithful and just and will forgive us our sins and purify us from all unrighteousness.
—1 JOHN 1:8-9

I was always able to look at the sins, wrongdoings, or mistakes of others. I was able to elaborate on how others affected me. I began looking at my own actions and behaviors. I saw how they had affected others.

I began correcting my behavior and became less judgmental of others. I am much lighter, freer, and happier. It wasn't pleasant going through this growing process, but the result has been worth it.

July 18

The Spirit you received does not make you slaves, so that you live in fear again; rather, the Spirit you received brought about your adoption to sonship. And by him we cry, "Abba, Father."
—ROMANS 8:15

Before I received the spirit of God. I was a slave to alcohol, drugs, cigarettes, sex, shopping, men, material things, and anything I thought would make my insides feel better. After all attempts of looking outside to fix my insides, I found I just needed to feed and water my spirit with spiritual food.

July 19

Then you will know the truth, and the truth will set you free.
—JOHN 8:32

The truth is God loves me. He has forgiven me for my past and future sins. I don't have to perform for Him. He loves and cares for me just as I am—bumps, lumps, bruises, zits, and boils. I am what I am.

July 20

Fixing our eyes on Jesus, the pioneer and perfecter of faith.
For the joy set before him he endured the cross, scorning its
shame, and sat down at the right hand of the throne of God.
—HEBREWS 12:2

I thank Jesus for loving me enough to come to earth and die for my sins. It would have been a sad state of affairs for me and everyone else on earth, if he hadn't. There isn't anyone among us who hasn't sinned. I have been saved from myself, from Satan, and from the world's version of what's important.

July 21

Who then is the one who condemns? No one. Christ Jesus who died—more than that, who was raised to life—is at the right hand of God and is also interceding for us.
—ROMANS 8:34

I have an intercessor who is always for me. He knows my heart and my desire to serve God. He loves me no matter what I have done. God hears and listens to his Son on my behalf.

July 22

"Come now, let us settle the matter," says the Lord. "Though your sins are like scarlet, they shall be as white as snow; though they are red as crimson, they shall be like wool."
—ISAIAH 1:18

I don't know how red I was, but I do know I wasn't white as wool. I had left a stain over my life and the lives of others. I know exactly when I accepted God into my life.

It was the first time I had been at peace in years. It was the same when I received the cancer diagnosis. Deep down, I knew all would be well in the end. God had this.

July 23

*For the sake of your name, Lord, forgive
my iniquity, though it is great.*
—PSALM 25:11

My mom and dad were well known in the community. I was ashamed of my behavior. I felt it was an embarrassment to them, and a sign of disrespect for all the sacrifices they made to give me a better life. My parents had already forgiven me, but I didn't understand.

Now, I am a parent. I am not embarrassed by my children's actions. I just want them to be happy and at peace. I don't like to see them make mistakes in their lives. I might get angry. I have already forgiven them no matter what they do.

The above verse is more for me than the Lord. He has already forgiven me, no matter what I have done. It's when I recognize my disrespect that I begin to get better by following the direction(s) of God.

July 24

Here I am! I stand at the door and knock. If anyone hears my voice and opens the door, I will come in and eat with that person, and they with me.
—REVELATION 3:20

There were many times I heard the knock, but I ignored it. I wanted to continue to live life my way. I thought this was easier.

It worked for a while, but eventually I opened the door because my way didn't work. I found it to be an easier way of living.

July 25

Simon answered, "Master, we've worked hard all night and haven't caught anything. But because you say so, I will let down the nets." When they had done so, they caught such a large number of fish that their nets began to break.
—LUKE 5:5-6

I haven't always had the faith Simon had at that moment. Jesus asked Simon to lower the net again. He expressed his doubt, but he did it anyway.

It reminds me when I first got sober. I met my sponsor. She told me, "I want you to pray every day for God to remove the desire and thoughts of drinking and drugging away from you."

I remember telling her, "Well, I just don't think that will work."

She said in a brash way, "I don't give a shit what you think that's what got you here in the first place."

I was desperate enough to do it. I didn't believe it would work, but I believed she believed it would. I did pray and have done it every day since then. I am still sober.

July 26

Therefore, there is now no condemnation
for those who are in Christ Jesus.
—ROMANS 8:1

I condemned myself on a daily basis, until Christ Jesus was sent here on earth.

I am not saying I don't beat myself up. I believe this is the human side of myself or the evil one. When the condemnation comes in my mind it's not of God.

When I was diagnosed with cancer my first thought, "I have cancer because I smoked for years." I had quit for over 14 years.

God still loves me. He still cares for me. He knows my faith will get me through this. He isn't condemning me.

July 27

*In him we were also chosen having been predestined
according to the plan of him who works out everything
in conformity with the purpose of his will.*
—Ephesians 1:11

I believe all of us were predestined. It is Satan who has free reign on this earth and bombards us with enticing thoughts. If we give in to the thoughts, they will lead only to a mental, spiritual, physical, or emotional death. It is only then God becomes a life preserver for us. He still loves us.

*He will wipe every tear from their eyes. There will
be no more death or mourning or crying or pain,
for the old order of things has passed away.*
—REVELATION 21:4

A scripture that gives me hope for the future. I will embrace the days of no more pain, death, or mourning. There is also hope for the present. The Bible instructs me how to obtain peace, love, and laughter, while living with pain and grief.

*To be made new in the attitude of your minds; and to put on the
new self, created to be like God in true righteousness and holiness.*
—EPHESIANS 4:23-24

I have this saying it all evens out in the end. If we do things which
aren't right, moral, or fair, my experience has been I will end up going
through the same thing with someone else.

I meditate on your precepts and consider your ways.
—PSALM 119:15

Once I began studying the scriptures, I learned about the love God has for me. He has given me chances just like I do as a parent. My kids can mess up, and I am always there for them.

My oldest child was crawling, and she was headed straight for a thumbtack on the floor. Just as she was about to pick it up and stick it in her mouth. I snatched it out of her hand. She wailed and cried. She didn't understand the big picture, but I did.

This is how God is with us. He knows what is good for us.

July 31

For everyone who asks receives; the one who seeks finds;
and to the one who knocks, the door will be opened.
—MATTHEW 7:8

At times I am too scared to ask because I am afraid of what the answer will be. I am too afraid to seek because of what I will find. Sometimes I am too afraid to knock because I am afraid the door won't open.

I always get an answer when I ask—yes, no, or wait. The answer can either come immediately, or take a long time. I might not be happy with what I find, but nothing can change until I begin to seek. When I knock the door has always opened. I just have to walk through.

August 1

The weapons we fight with are not the weapons of the world. On the contrary, they have divine power to demolish strongholds. We demolish arguments and every pretension that sets itself up against the knowledge of God, and we take captive every thought to make it obedient to Christ.
—2 CORINTHIANS 10:4-5

This world is bombarded with evil spirits ready to pounce on me like a hyena on a piece of meat. There are good spirits or angels, who will swoop me up like an eagle, which no evil force can touch. All I have to do is ask and believe.

Cancer to me is an evil force ready to eat my mind, body, and spirit at every opportunity. I have angels sent by the Lord, who will replenish me with courage, peace, and love.

August 2

Amen to that!!! I was diagnosed with lung cancer, and it had spread to my hip. After finishing my first round of treatments, the cancer had spread to the lymph nodes and then to my brain.

The human part of me thought, "I better get my affairs in order." The spiritual part of me knew God had this.

He is healing me as I sit here writing this. God has given me the ability to live my life relativity the same.

August 3

give thanks in all circumstances; for this is
God's will for you in Christ Jesus.
—1THESSALONIANS 5:18

It includes the cancer, and the radiation, chemotherapy, immunotherapy, shots for my bones, operations, the side effects, and my family and friends. Most days I do give thanks for my circumstances.

August 4

The Spirit himself testifies with our spirit that we are God's children.
—ROMANS 8:16

Our spirits converse with each other over what is good or bad for me; what can teach me a lesson; and what I can learn from life. I can use all to share my experience, strength, and hope.

August 5

So Pharaoh said to Joseph, "I hereby put you in charge of the whole land of Egypt." Then Pharaoh took his signet ring from his finger and put it on Joseph's finger. He dressed him in robes of fine linen and put a gold chain around his neck. He had him ride in a chariot as his second-in-command, and people shouted before him, "make way." Thus he put him in charge of the whole land of Egypt.
—Genesis 41:41-43

Joseph was thrown into the pit, drawn out of it, and sold into slavery. Joseph overcame all these adversities and more because of his belief in God's goodness. He had faith all would work out in his life.

There are days when I question how much more I can go through. I think of Joseph, and what he lived through. He didn't give up. He put one foot in front of the other trusting God all the way. He is an example I often look up to when I am discouraged.

August 6

*And when you pray, do not keep on babbling like pagans, for
they think they will be heard because of their many words.*
—Matthew 6:7

There are certain things I pray for each day. I often wonder if God gets tired of hearing the same thing over and over again. I believe we need to pray daily, just like we eat and drink daily.

I journal every morning. This is when I give God all of my concerns, fears, accomplishments, struggles, and victories. I believe God knows my heart. He hears my prayers in whatever form they are.

August 7

They will see his face, and his name will be on their foreheads.
—REVELATION 22:4

This is something to look forward too. I will be totally and completely with God. I will be in spirit, but I will be whole.

August 8

With God we will gain the victory, and he
will trample down our enemies.
—Psalm 60:12

I shouldn't have been able to do or survived many of the things I already have such as alcohol, drugs, cigarettes, marriages, and severe allergies. The list could go on and on.

Why shouldn't God be able to trample this cancer?

August 9

This is how love is made complete among us so that we will have confidence on the day of judgment: In this world we are like Jesus.
—1 JOHN 4:17

Love is much more peaceful for me and my soul than hate. When I love, and know I am loved by Jesus it's easier to love others and myself. It's like a continuous circle.

August 10

*Trust in the Lord with all your heart and lean not
on your own understanding; in all your ways submit
to him, and he will make your paths straight.*
—PROVERBS 3:5-6

If I lean on my own understanding, I am doomed. I don't have the capacity to understand the big picture, even though I think I do. God sees and knows all.

This is where faith comes in. My own experience has taught me when I do trust and have faith it will be for my good.

August 11

As Jesus went on from there, he saw a man named
Matthew sitting at the tax collector's booth. "Follow me,"
he told him, and Matthew got up and followed him.
—MATTHEW 9:9

Tax collectors were even more despised and prone to dishonesty during that time. For Jesus to even consider and ask Matthew to be a disciple shows me he can and does perform miracles.

August 12

*He replied, "Blessed rather are those who
hear the word of God and obey it."*
—LUKE 11:28

I am at much more peace when I am living God's word, no matter
my circumstances.

August 13

Humble yourselves before the Lord, and he will lift you up.
—JAMES 4:10

Without the Lord I am nothing, and I can't do anything. It's only through the power of the Lord that I am still here—living and learning.

August 14

The Lord is in his holy temple; the Lord is on his heavenly throne. He observes everyone on earth; his eyes examine them.
—PSALM 11:4

God looks at the actions of the good and the evil. God uses people, places, and things meant for my harm and turns them around for my good. The cancer meant to harm me will be used by God to spread his word.

August 15

One day Jesus was praying in a certain place. When he finished, one of his disciples said to him, "Lord, teach us to pray, just as John taught his disciples."
—LUKE 11:1

The Lord's Prayer is very powerful. It really covers everything. This prayer can become rote, and I am just reciting it. I believe God wants to have a relationship with me. How do I do this?

I talk to him as a friend, but I also listen. I hear him through my soul, friends, strangers, and circumstances. God gives me answers every day. Sometimes the answers come much later than the questions. I have a relationship with God.

I was grateful when the cancer was diagnosed. I had a relationship with God. I had many questions, and many answers have come.

August 16

If anyone acknowledges that Jesus is the Son of God, God lives in them and they in God.
—1 JOHN 4:15

All I have to do is admit Jesus is the Son of God, and I have a relationship with him. He works through me daily. I still have a problem working in God. I can't imagine God wanting me. I can imagine working for God. This is exactly what I am doing.

August 17

"I am the Lord's servant," Mary answered. "May your word to me be fulfilled." Then the angel left her.
—LUKE 1:38

God has spoken to me. I knew I would live for many more years when I was diagnosed with cancer. Why? Because I knew God wasn't finished with me yet.

I knew I was to share my experience, strength, and hope of how God has worked in my life since the cancer diagnosis. How my relationship with God has changed and has become much deeper because of it.

August 18

After leaving them, he went up on a mountainside to pray.
—MARK 6:46

Jesus needed time to be alone with his Father. He needed time for guidance, to strengthen himself for the days ahead, and to feed his spirit and soul. We all need this time.

August 19

Jesus said, "Let the little children come to me, and do not hinder
them, for the kingdom of heaven belongs to such as these."
—MATTHEW 19:14

Children have questions, and trust the answers given to them. Sometimes the answers are, "Because I said so." There isn't really an explanation. They just know it is so.

Children trust the parent or grown up, and they move on.

This is how I need to be with God. I think this is what Jesus was trying to teach me in this story. When I found out I had cancer I had to trust God had the answers. I might not even know what the questions are, but I know God does have the answers.

August 20

On my account you will be brought before governors and kings as witnesses to them and to the Gentiles.
—Matthew 10:18

Jesus is telling them beforehand what will happen. This serves many purposes to prepare them for what is to come, and they would remember him telling them this. It is a prophecy.

He has done with us the same. He tells us there will be many trials and tribulations, but it will be all worth it. We will literally live in the house of the Lord.

August 21

*There is neither Jew nor Gentile, neither slave nor free, nor is
there male and female, for you are all one in Christ Jesus.*
—GALATIANS 3:28

Christ doesn't discriminate. He uses us all for his purpose. He doesn't
see color, race, nor sex. All he sees is our heart and intention.

August 22

Accept one another, then, just as Christ accepted
you, in order to bring praise to God.
—ROMANS 15:7

I have been guilty of not accepting others. There was one person who I judged, and I couldn't find one good quality about him. I even told others he was really Satan in disguise.

I saw him shortly before his death. He looked awful, not just physically, but spiritually and mentally too. He looked as if he were in turmoil. I was filled with sadness and grief for him, and I was able to forgive him for all he had done to others.

Our eyes met, and not a word needed to be said. The funny thing, he never once tried to deceive me like he had others. I had been protected. After his death, I was grateful I came to peace with him. I pray I receive forgiveness from others—either known or unknown.

August 23

Jesus entered the temple courts and drove out all who were buying and selling there. He overturned the tables of the money changers and the benches of those selling doves. "It is written," he said to them. "My house will be called a house of prayer, but you are making it a den of robbers."
—MATTHEW 21:12-13

This gives me hope. It shows Jesus was angry because people had abused or made a mockery of his house. Even Jesus wasn't exempt from the human emotion of anger. This gives me permission to be human. Sometimes it is alright to get angry when someone is abusing me, another person, or the house of God. It is alright to speak up.

August 24

And so we know and rely on the love God has for us. God is love. Whoever lives in love lives in God, and God in them.
—1 JOHN 4:16

What is love? An intense feeling of deep affection, fondness, tenderness, warmth, intimacy, attachment, endearment, devotion, adoration, doting, idolization, worship, passion, desire, yearning, compassion, care, concern, friendship, kindness, charity, goodwill, sympathy, altruism, unselfishness, benevolence, and humanity. As I do for others, he does unto me.

August 25

He will turn the hearts of the parents to their children,
and the hearts of the children to their parents; or else I
will come and strike the land with total destruction.
—MALACHI 4:6

We are to honor and respect each other—no matter what.

August 26

I will betroth you to me forever; I will betroth you in righteousness and justice, in love and compassion. I will betroth you in faithfulness, and you will acknowledge the Lord.
—HOSEA 2:19-20

This is a promise from God to us. Even though we are to be over the animals I can't say what I would do if confronted by a bear, giraffe, or snake.

I am scared some days of the cancer, but God has it all. I am betrothed to God. As the saying goes, "It's all good."

August 27

But his subjects hated him and sent a delegation after
him to say, "We don't want this man to be our king."
—LUKE 19:14

It really didn't matter what the delegation or people wanted, Gentile or Jew. Jesus was going to be king in this life and the next. He is the King of Kings and Lord of Lords. God will have his way.

August 28

Gracious words are a honeycomb, sweet to
the soul and healing to the bones.
—Proverbs 16:24

My mom used to tell me, "You can get more with honey than vinegar." I have often told my youngest daughter this. I have observed people will do more, if I compliment instead of criticizing them.

August 29

*After he had dismissed them, he went up on a mountainside
by himself to pray. Later that night, he was there alone.*
—Matthew 14:23

We all need time alone with God. I have to be alone with him to begin
my day. He strengthens me. He guides me. Throughout the day, he leads
me where I am to go.

August 30

It is good to praise the Lord and make music to
your name, O Most High proclaiming your love in
the morning and your faithfulness at night.
—Psalm 92:1-2

I praise the Lord. Living with cancer means some days are better than others. God has it all in his hands. I know this to the core of my being.

August 31

So shall thy poverty come as one that travelleth;
and thy want as an armed man.
—Proverbs 24:34

It is a sad when our soul is drained of anything good. We have to guard our soul like an armed man. If we don't, we won't be able to face life's trials and tribulations.

September 1

The men turned away and went toward Sodom, but
Abraham remained standing before the Lord.
—GENESIS 18:22

God spared Abraham because he had the ultimate faith. He trusted God without question. I try to do this day to day, minute to minute, and sometimes second to second. I trust God with the cancer.

September 2

Because you are his sons, God sent the Spirit of his Son
into our hearts, the Spirit who calls out, "Abba, Father."
—GALATIANS 4:6

I called out to God with everything I had in me and gave my life to him. I became part of God's family. All along it has been an illusion I was controlling my life.

September 3

Now to him who is able to do immeasurably more than all we ask or imagine, according to his power that is at work within us, to him be glory in the church and in Christ Jesus throughout all generations, for ever and ever! Amen.
—Ephesians 3:20-21

All I wanted when I landed in AA was not to drink or drug anymore. If I had settled just for this, I would have cut myself far short. Through my ever-growing relationship with God I have been given so much more than I deserve. I have been shown how merciful God is.

Come near to God and he will come near to you. Wash your hands, you sinners, and purify your hearts, you double-minded.
—JAMES 4:8

I haven't been disappointed every time I have drawn near to God. I am not saying the solutions or answers come right away. I give them to God, and his answers might be different than what I expected.

When I am double-minded I live in turmoil, and I question everything. When I trust then I am at peace.

Dear children, let us not love with words or
speech but with actions and in truth.
—1 JOHN 3:18

I was diagnosed with cancer, and I realized how many warm-hearted, loving, and sincere people were in the world. I had become callous, hardened, and cynical. I focused on the negative, and my mind, body, soul, and spirit were paying for it.

Today, the positive changes in me, which have resulted from me having cancer, are my attitudes and actions towards others. I pray others. I send cards and text messages. I make phone calls. I visit. I have seen an action as small as a mustard seed have a transforming effect for all involved.

September 6

Now I am about to go the way of all the earth. You know with all your heart and soul that not one of all the good promises the Lord your God gave you has failed. Every promise has been fulfilled; not one has failed.
—JOSHUA 23:14

All of us must die. There is no way out of this journey. We have to leave to arrive at our new destination. This is the way it is and has always been. We knew this upfront.

God gave us this world and all the good in it. He let us have the experiences of seeing the sunset, smelling the beach, feeling the touch of someone's hand, and hearing someone laughing. We still have to go.

It's hard to imagine a better place. I think of how evil has taken over so many hearts and souls. When it's time for me to leave I won't have to experience or think about evil again.

September 7

And if by grace, then it cannot be based on works;
if it were, grace would no longer be grace.
—ROMANS 11:6

Oh, how true this is. None of us deserve to be part of God's family. We are all sinners. When we realize this God's grace can enter into our souls, and we begin to change by serving him and spreading the word to others.

God's grace continues to transform my life.

September 8

Do not judge, or you too will be judged. For in the same way you judge others, you will be judged, and with the measure you use, it will be measured to you.
—MATTHEW 7:1-2

My experience has been, if I judge someone, guess what? I will be experiencing it down the road. After much heartache I then understood how they came to their decision.

I am not so quick to judge now. It doesn't mean I still don't. I am human. I don't know what is right or wrong for another person. I am not God.

September 9

When I heard these things, I sat down and wept. For some days
I mourned and fasted and prayed before the God of heaven.
—NEHEMIAH 1:4

God is with me through my grief and pleas for mercy. I know God is my source, and the only source to bring healing to any situation. I am not blind any longer, and I can't pretend to be.

September 10

Trust in the Lord forever, for the Lord, the
Lord himself, is the Rock eternal.
—ISAIAH 26:4

Two malignant brain tumors were found, and they were taken out. I then had radiation on my brain. During this time the doctors and nurses looked and sounded solemn. It made me take a step back.

My family and support system were offering help. They were saying how sorry they were, and they were praying for me. This made me take another step back.

I trusted in God. He showed his power by working through me. I have been given an unending supply of peace and strength during this cancer journey.

September 11

And having disarmed the powers and authorities, he made a
public spectacle of them, triumphing over them by the cross.
—COLOSSIANS 2:15

God showed all of us he was the one and only one. He has the power, and he is the source.

September 12

About eight days after Jesus said this, he took Peter, John and James with him and went up onto a mountain to pray.
—LUKE 9:28

Jesus wanted to show them he was the Son of God. They saw, felt, heard, and believed. When they witnessed the events that took place their belief was sealed. They still had human doubts.

When I found out I had cancer I had my doubts if God would be able to handle this! Once I gave it all to him it has been handled.

September 13

Ask and it will be given to you; seek and you will find; knock and the door will be opened to you. For everyone who asks receives; the one who seeks finds; and to the one who knocks, the door will be opened.
—MATTHEW 7:7-8

If my children ask me for anything, I will do whatever is in my power to give it to them. I might also feel, spiritually, they aren't ready, or they might need to learn a lesson.

My Father in Heaven does the same for me. The door is always open. All I have to do is knock. The answers come, sometimes in unexpected ways.

September 14

*Start children off on the way they should go, and even
when they are old they will not turn from it.*
—PROVERBS 22:6

I was introduced to God at a young age. I tried to run like Jonah, but to no avail. When I returned God landed me in AA. I believe this was the only way I was able to find a God of my understanding and begin to develop a spiritual relationship with him.

My children know I pray every day. They have witnessed me praying over them for God's protection. They would roll their eyes, but I didn't care because I know the power of God. Now, they do too.

September 15

Finally, brothers and sisters, whatever is true, whatever is noble, whatever is right, whatever is pure, whatever is lovely, whatever is admirable—if anything is excellent or praiseworthy—think about such things. Whatever you have learned or received or heard from me, or seen in me—put it into practice. And the God of peace will be with you.
—PHILIPPIANS 4:8-9

I have worried; obsessed; projected; had conversations in my head; been double-minded; lived in fear; acted out in anger; and experienced extreme anxiety. My way of thinking changed with God's power.

I think about the way the scripture says life is to be lived, and it is a more peaceful way of life. I believe I had to go through the negative to appreciate the positive.

September 16

"Father, if you are willing, remove this cup from me. Nevertheless, not my will, but yours, be done." And there appeared to him an angel from heaven, strengthening him. And being in agony he prayed more earnestly; and his sweat became like great drops of blood falling down to the ground. And when he rose from prayer, he came to the disciples and found them sleeping for sorrow, and he said to them, "Why are you sleeping? Rise and pray that you may not enter into temptation."
—LUKE 22:39-46

I hear other people say Jesus was perfect. This scripture shows me it isn't so. He had great fear, trepidation, and anger. It was the human part of him. I am presently human.

I also have the spirit in me just like Jesus had his Father in him. He was willing to do what his Father asked of him in spite of how he felt. Faith and trust in action.

Very early in the morning, while it was still dark, Jesus got up,
left the house and went off to a solitary place, where he prayed.
—MARK 1:35

If I feel lost or out of sorts, this means I haven't had enough time with God. My day is much easier when I begin it with God.

I found out I had cancer, and I was so grateful I had been praying for years. I knew God would use this for his glory.

It is never too late to develop a relationship with God.

September 18

I will not leave you as orphans; I will come to you.
—JOHN 14:18

I feel comforted the most when I have experienced trials. I usually don't realize this until the trial is over. I am God's child.

September 19

Come, let us bow down in worship, let us kneel before the Lord our Maker; for he is our God and we are the people of his pasture, the flock under his care. Today, if only you would hear his voice.
—PSALM 95:6-7

My praise goes to the Lord. He has the power. He is the source.

September 20

May you be blessed by the Lord, the Maker of heaven and earth.
—PSALM 115:15

The Lord has blessed me beyond my wildest dreams. If I had just settled for what I thought would be best for me, I would have sold myself far too short. I have what I was looking for all along with the drugs, alcohol, and cigarettes.

September 21

When Jesus saw this, he was indignant. He said to them, "Let the little children come to me, and do not hinder them, for the kingdom of God belongs to such as these. Truly I tell you, anyone who will not receive the kingdom of God like a little child will never enter it."
—MARK 10:14-15

Jesus wants us just like little children. Faithful beyond a doubt; trusting; innocent; and malleable. With these qualities he can shape me to show others his love.

September 22

Better is one day in your courts than a thousand elsewhere;
I would rather be a doorkeeper in the house of my God than
dwell in the tents of the wicked. For the Lord God is a sun
and shield; the Lord bestows favor and honor; no good thing
does he withhold from those whose walk is blameless.
—PSALM 84:10-11

When I would move to a new home I would pack my diplomas.

I found out I had cancer and realized what was important. I asked myself, "When I am gone who is going to want these? What would they do with them?"

What I thought was so important wasn't. The education, yes, but not the sheepskin. What I had earned no one could take away from me.

Living with the wicked I used the sheepskin to show everyone what I had done. With God he loves me with or without the sheepskin.

September 23

*Far above all rule and authority, power and dominion,
and every name that is invoked, not only in the
present age but also in the one to come.*
—EPHESIANS 1:21

He is above it all—everyone and everything. Praise God!

September 24

This, then, is how you should pray: Our Father in heaven, hallowed be your name, your kingdom come, your will be done, on earth as it is in heaven. Give us today our daily bread. And forgive us our debts, as we also have forgiven our debtors, and lead us not into temptation, but deliver us from the evil one. For if you forgive other people when they sin against you, your heavenly Father will also forgive you. But if you do not forgive others their sins, your Father will not forgive your sins.
—MATTHEW 6:9-15

Jesus gave us a prayer. He kept it simple, but it is a prayer that covers everything from food to forgiveness. This prayer has gotten me through many rough patches.

September 25

*Then I acknowledged my sin to you and did not cover
up my iniquity. I said, "I will confess my transgressions
to the Lord." And you forgave the guilt of my sin.*
—PSALM 32:5

It is freeing when I confess my wrong. It saves me from the yucky feelings, which show up when I am trying hide a sin. When exposed to the light the sin vanishes, and God forgives. If kept in the dark it grows like mold, and it becomes a barrier between God and me.

September 26

My heart says of you, "Seek his face!" Your face, Lord, I will seek.
—PSALM 27:8

The Lord wants to have a relationship with me. All I have to do is go to him to talk and to listen. I can talk to him about anything. I can either talk out loud, in silent prayer, or by journaling. It doesn't matter to the Lord my method of communication. He is always there to listen and to answer.

September 27

He said to the Israelites, "In the future when your descendants ask their parents, 'What do these stones mean?' tell them, 'Israel crossed the Jordan on dry ground.' For the Lord your God dried up the Jordan before you until you had crossed over. The Lord your God did to the Jordan what he had done to the Red Sea when he dried it up before us until we had crossed over."
—JOSHUA 4:21-23

I interpret this as I am to tell and show my children what God has done for me and others. The reason is so I won't forget all he has done for me. God is showing me how to live with cancer and to continue to live my life.

September 28

The Lord is near to all who call on him,
to all who call on him in truth.
—Psalm 145:18

All the Lord expects of me is to be truthful with him. He knows what is best for me. There are some days I am fearful of the cancer, and what it is doing to my body and my family. I either talk with God or others about it. I know God is listening, and I can feel his reassuring presence.

September 29

Joshua fought the Amalekites as Moses had ordered, and Moses,
Aaron and Hur went to the top of the hill. As long as Moses
held up his hands, the Israelites were winning, but whenever he
lowered his hands, the Amalekites were winning. When Moses'
hands grew tired, they took a stone and put it under him and he
sat on it. Aaron and Hur held his hands up—one on one side,
one on the other—so that his hands remained steady till sunset.
So Joshua overcame the Amalekite army with the sword.
—Exodus 17:10-13

Faith is all about believing in the unbelievable. When we do miracles begin to happen.

I remember I was getting fluids. I had been getting sick to my stomach. It was because I had two tumors pressing on my brain.

There was a guy sitting across from me. He stopped in front of my chair before leaving. He was talking about God, and that it was all good. I can't remember everything he said, but I knew he was from God.

He was just an ordinary guy, but his soul was extraordinary. He brightened my day.

September 30

Do you not know? Have you not heard? The Lord is the everlasting God, the Creator of the ends of the earth. He will not grow tired or weary, and his understanding no one can fathom. He gives strength to the weary and increases the power of the weak. Even youths grow tired and weary, and young men stumble and fall; but those who hope in the Lord will renew their strength. They will soar on wings like eagles; they will run and not grow weary, they will walk and not be faint.
—ISAIAH 40:28-31

I have lived these words, and I will continue to, until I go to the other side. Before I had my fourth surgery, I was beginning to question how much my body could endure. I didn't have a choice in the matter, unless I wanted to stay in excruciating pain and be miserable.

I prayed, journaled, talked with others, suited up, and showed up. I had the surgery. Less than a week later, I feel better.

October 1

If you remain in me and my words remain in you, ask
whatever you wish, and it will be done for you.
—JOHN 15:7

I had to have my second Magnetic Resonance Imaging (MRI). Even with earplugs in my ears, a mask on my face, and foam around the sides of my head I heard the racket and all the weird sounds. I was petrified.

What did I do? I would spell the "Serenity Prayer," The Lord's Prayer," and my own prayers. I got through the MRI with God and my husband by my side.

October 2

Praise be to the God and Father of our Lord Jesus Christ,
the Father of compassion and the God of all comfort.
—2 CORINTHIANS 1:3

All praises go to God and the Father of our Lord Jesus Christ. He is the one who creates us. He is the one who heals us. He is the one who loves us. He is the only one.

Keep your lives free from the love of money and be content with what you have, because God has said, "Never will I leave you; never will I forsake you." So we say with confidence, "The Lord is my helper; I will not be afraid. What can mere mortals do to me?"
—HEBREWS 13:5-6

When I was younger much of my security and identity was wrapped up in what I had; what I had to show for being here on earth; what I had accomplished; what my achievements were; and what I did for a living.

Life had its way with me. What used to work for me didn't any longer. There wasn't any peace in my soul.

My journey took a detour back to the beginning; back to my roots; back to my spiritual self; back to the one who created me; and back to the place where the ultimate peace lies.

I felt that God had abandoned me. I found that God never did leave me. He was always there waiting on me.

October 4

Now when Joshua was near Jericho, he looked up and saw
a man standing in front of him with a drawn sword in his
hand. Joshua went up to him and asked, "Are you for us or
for our enemies?" "Neither," he replied, "but as commander
of the army of the Lord I have now come." Then Joshua
fell facedown to the ground in reverence, and asked him,
"What message does my Lord have for his servant?"
—JOSHUA 5:13-14

I was in a grocery store overwhelmed with raising my two children as a single parent. I was hoping they would be alright. We were in the cereal section, and this lady appeared out of nowhere. She had the whitest hair, the calmest demeanor, and the brightest blue eyes

She said to me, "I see your children will be fine."

I remember asking myself. 'How did she know what I was thinking?' She was then gone. This gave me the push I needed to continue.

My children both graduated from college. I have a granddaughter. They have loving and giving hearts. They know it's ok to make mistakes. They have been allowed to find their own spiritual journey. They have learned a lot of this from our journey together.

October 5

*I urge, then, first of all, that petitions, prayers, intercession
and thanksgiving be made for all people—for kings
and all those in authority, that we may live peaceful
and quiet lives in all godliness and holiness.*
—1 TIMOTHY 2:1-2

I really don't know what is best for others. I can see how many times I have been wrong.

Now, I ask God for his will to be done in the lives of others. This keeps it out of my hands, where it tends to get all twisted up.

October 6

as far as the east is from the west, so far has he
removed our transgressions from us.
—Psalm 103:12

God has removed all of my transgressions, every single one of them, totally. I am blessed and free.

October 7

Now if the foot should say, "Because I am not a hand, I do not belong to the body," it would not for that reason stop being part of the body. And if the ear should say, "Because I am not an eye, I do not belong to the body," it would not for that reason stop being part of the body. If the whole body were an eye, where would the sense of hearing be? If the whole body were an ear, where would the sense of smell be? But in fact God has placed the parts in the body, every one of them, just as he wanted them to be.
—1 Corinthians 12:15-18

We are all needed to become one of a whole. God made it this way. If God wanted it to be different, it would have been. He designed us to need, desire, and want to be around others.

One person might have the gift of being an excellent speaker, while another is an excellent writer. We are all needed to complete God's will. He needs us all, not just one or two of us.

October 8

I, even I, am he who blots out your transgressions, for
my own sake, and remembers your sins no more.
—Isaiah 43:25

God would rather look at our capacity as humans to spread love, peace, and good cheer rather than our capacity for making mistakes. Why does God do this? Because he created us for good.

October 9

He does not treat us as our sins deserve or
repay us according to our iniquities.
—Psalm 103:10

My past condemned me to a life sentence of guilt, remorse, worry, fear, and no forgiveness. I received mercy, grace, unconditional love, and forgiveness when I turned my life over to God. If I got what deserved, I wouldn't be sitting here writing this.

October 10

They put a purple robe on him, then twisted together
a crown of thorns and set it on him. And they began
to call out to him, "Hail, king of the Jews!"
—MARK 15:17-18

This scripture speaks to me on many different levels. They could do with him whatever they wanted. It didn't matter because God was going to have his way. It had already been foretold.

These men running around putting a crown of thorns on Jesus' head was an illusion of control. It shows we will do anything to someone or something we don't understand.

Really who has the power? Jesus was born, and he changed the world and mankind. My life isn't my own any longer.

October 11

Give, and it will be given to you. A good measure, pressed down, shaken together and running over, will be poured into your lap. For with the measure you use, it will be measured to you.
—LUKE 6:38

When I was diagnosed with cancer, I began to wonder how I was going to get to places because I couldn't drive. I didn't want to be a burden on other's or my family.

Friends began to volunteer to bring me food, and signed up to take me to chemotherapy, radiation, meetings, or any other place I needed to go. I couldn't believe it.

I was trying to understand why people were being so nice. I certainly didn't feel I was a giver. I realized I might not be able to give as they did, but I do give in my own way. God saw this, and this verse became and still is a reality for me.

October 12

I think of taking a nice, hot, clean shower, and then putting my stinky, dirty clothes back on. I might feel better for a while, but not as long as I would if I had some good, fresh, and clean clothes on.

I am continuously having to be put into a new wineskin because I am not the same as I was ten, twenty, or thirty years ago.

October 13

*Follow God's example, therefore, as dearly loved children
and walk in the way of love, just as Christ loved us and gave
himself up for us as a fragrant offering and sacrifice to God.*
—EPHESIANS 5:1-2

I just wrote a friend who lives in another state. Deep down we became friends due to a basic survival bond, and I am so grateful she has continued to be a part of my life.

She literally just lost the love of her life a few hours ago. I wrote this to her, "Know there is NO separation in love." I don't know where it came from.

I knew deep down in my being I was supposed to send the message to her just like I knew I was to write this daily meditation book.

October 14

The Lord is my rock, my fortress and my deliverer;
my God is my rock, in whom I take refuge, my shield
and the horn of my salvation, my stronghold.
—PSALM 18:2

A rock to me is immoveable. The only way it can be moved is through a force of nature or some divine intervention. I take refuge and comfort in knowing this. Now, with more time and experience I do realize that God is my rock and refuge.

They came to Bethsaida, and some people brought a blind man and begged Jesus to touch him. He took the blind man by the hand and led him outside the village. When he had spit on the man's eyes and put his hands on him, Jesus asked, "Do you see anything?" He looked up and said, "I see people; they look like trees walking around." Once more Jesus put his hands on the man's eyes. Then his eyes were opened, his sight was restored, and he saw everything clearly.
—MARK 8:22-25

Jesus had to perform miracles for us to believe he was the Messiah. Jesus also knew our human nature. We would be spreading the word of these miracles, which trickled down to us.

The miracle and healing power of redemption for our life to be instantly changed and to live a life of eternity with our Lord.

October 16

*Again, truly I tell you that if two of you on earth
agree about anything they ask for, it will be done for
them by my Father in heaven. For where two or three
gather in my name, there am I with them.*
—MATTHEW 18:19-20

I have been to many AA meetings where there were only two to three of us present. Some of those meetings were the most powerful and intimate instead of the larger ones. I felt a deep connection between those in the meeting, and a definite healing and guiding presence of God. I realize God loves me, and he is always available.

October 17

Dear friends, now we are children of God, and what we will be has not yet been made known. But we know that when Christ appears, we shall be like him, for we shall see him as he is.
—1 JOHN 3:2

I might have a preconceived idea of how things will be with me spiritually or physically, but I really don't know. God knows, and this is all that matters.

October 18

*"Honor your father and mother"—which is the
first commandment with a promise.*
—EPHESIANS 6:2

I began smoking as a teenager. My dad smoked. I thought, "Why couldn't I?" He found out I was smoking. He said he wished I would try to quit. I finally did when I was forty-four years old. My dad was diagnosed with stage IV lung cancer. He lived nine months with treatments.

Flash forward fourteen years—I now have stage IV lung cancer. If I hadn't quit smoking, this could have happened much sooner to me.

Since 2005, science has come a long way. God is the God of second chances.

October 19

*I have other sheep that are not of this sheep pen. I
must bring them also. They too will listen to my voice,
and there shall be one flock and one shepherd.*
—JOHN 10:16

Jesus was sent down here to gather all his sheep. Some of us have strayed much further than others. Jesus doesn't give up on his own.

Thank God he didn't give up on me.

October 20

But when you give to the needy, do not let your left hand know what your right hand is doing, so that your giving may be in secret. Then your Father, who sees what is done in secret, will reward you.
—MATTHEW 6:3-4

It feels good to give in secret. It has its own reward. No hoopla, no bragging, just from the heart.

October 21

Search me, O God, and know my heart; test me and know my anxious thoughts. See if there is any offensive way in me, and lead me in the way everlasting.
—PSALM 139:23-24

My experience with this verse can be pleasant or not so pleasant. I want this in my heart and mind, but, truthfully, I don't want to be picked and prodded. I especially don't want it to be mentally, spiritually, or physically painful. Once it is over, there is a peace that transcends it all.

October 22

Greater love has no one than this: to lay
down one's life for one's friends.
—JOHN 15:13

Why is this? Because this is what Jesus did for us. He gave his very life so we may live. The ultimate sacrifice for which I am eternally grateful.

October 23

Then God said to Abraham, "As for you, you must keep my covenant, you and your descendants after you for the generations to come. This is my covenant with you and your descendants after you, the covenant you are to keep: Every male among you shall be circumcised. You are to undergo circumcision, and it will be the sign of the covenant between me and you."
—GENESIS 17:9-11

God is a man of his word. If we keep our part of the agreement, God will take care of his portion. He told Abraham what would happen and will continue to happen until the end of time.

Jesus told us. If we are baptized, trust in him, and do unto others, we would have everlasting life and peace. What gifts!!!

October 24

*May God himself, the God of peace, sanctify you through
and through. May your whole spirit, soul and body be kept
blameless at the coming of our Lord Jesus Christ.*
—1 Thessalonians 5:23

God is the only one who can keep me safe and peaceful. I have tried
other avenues, but to no avail. The other ways were only temporary fixes.
God, Lord Jesus Christ, and the Holy Spirit are the permanent solutions.

October 25

Submit yourselves, then, to God. Resist the devil, and he will flee from you.
—James 4:7

I remember when I asked in Jesus' name for Satan to get behind me, and it worked. I haven't stopped saying this simple prayer. It doesn't matter to me what others' think.

Two blind men were sitting by the roadside, and when
they heard that Jesus was going by, they shouted,
"Lord, Son of David, have mercy on us!"
—MATTHEW 20:29-30

What faith!!! They couldn't see, but they believed that Jesus could enable them to see. Jesus is able to do anything.

October 27

Who is it that overcomes the world? Only the one
who believes that Jesus is the Son of God.
—1 JOHN 5:5

This world is only temporary. When I have put all my hopes and dreams in this world or lost sight of the spiritual realm, it has always led to my ultimate downfall. Jesus is the answer.

October 28

In him you were also circumcised with a circumcision not performed by human hands. Your whole self ruled by the flesh was put off when you were circumcised by Christ.
—Colossians 2:11

I remember when I turned my will and life over to the care of the God of my understanding. My most glaring defects of character were removed. I experienced such peace and tranquility I had never known before.

The desires and thoughts of drinking and drugging were removed from me at once. Over time, Christ pruned me. He got rid of what wasn't needed for his purpose.

October 29

*O God, my heart is fixed; I will sing and
give praise, even with my glory.*
—PSALM 108:1

When my soul is happy. I sing, hum, and have a little kick in my step.

October 30

Therefore, my dear brothers and sisters, stand firm. Let nothing move you. Always give yourselves fully to the work of the Lord, because you know that your labor in the Lord is not in vain.
—1 CORINTHIANS 15:58

I like how God gave us encouraging words either directly or indirectly from him. He knew we would be going through some tough times, and we would want to give up five minutes before the miracle happened.

God left us Paul's letters. He left us the Bible. He left us the Holy Spirit. He left us each other.

October 31

The Lord will fight for you; you need only to be still.
—Exodus 14:14

God does fight my battles. The problem is I have to let him. My human nature is to try and fight my own battles, as well as others. God is a much more experienced warrior than me.

He is fighting my cancer. All I have to do is trust him and show up.

November 1

Be alert and of sober mind. Your enemy the devil prowls around like a roaring lion looking for someone to devour.
—1 PETER 5:8

When I think the battle is over is when I get pounced upon like a rag doll. I have to continuously be vigilant against the enemy. He wants my soul. The cancer has been a learning experience of God's power not Satan's.

November 2

Glorify the Lord with me; let us exalt his name together.
—Psalm 34:3

I remember when I was going through a very tough time. I was beating myself up because I was full of fear and terror, and I was having to depend on others.

A friend of mind told me, "It's always better when we do things together than by ourselves." This was one of the best things she could have ever said to me. I am not supposed to do this alone.

When the trumpets sounded, the army shouted, and at the sound of the trumpet, when the men gave a loud shout, the wall collapsed; so everyone charged straight in, and they took the city.
—JOSHUA 6:20

The power of God—noise made the walls fall down, and a city captured. God has the power to conquer cancer.

November 4

*If it is possible, as far as it depends on
you, live at peace with everyone.*
—ROMANS 12:18

I am much more comfortable in my own skin when I am at peace with others. I have squandered my life away living with unforgiveness, regrets, sorrows, anger, and fear. This wore my soul down. Living the other way lifts my own and others' souls.

November 5

Therefore, if you are offering your gift at the altar and there remember that your brother or sister has something against you, leave your gift there in front of the altar. First go and be reconciled to them; then come and offer your gift.
—MATTHEW 5:23-24

Our relationships with each other are very important according to this scripture. In the end, isn't this all that matters, our relationships?

November 6

Why, my soul, are you downcast? Why so disturbed within me? Put your hope in God, for I will yet praise him, my Savior and my God.
—PSALM 42:5

My answer has always come from the Lord. He is my source. He has the power to change an incident 360° in less than a second to our benefit.

November 7

Therefore confess your sins to each other and pray
for each other so that you may be healed. The prayer
of a righteous person is powerful and effective.
—JAMES 5:16

There was no healing or forgiveness until I could honestly look at myself. I did this by confessing my shortcomings to another person. It was easier for me to forgive others.

November 8

But he knows the way that I take; when he has
tested me, I will come forth as gold.
—Job 23:10

There is something comforting deep down knowing someone is on my side no matter what. It gives me a deep, resounding peace in my soul. He hasn't forsaking me during this cancer journey.

November 9

*Whoever walks in integrity walks securely, but
whoever takes crooked paths will be found out.*
—PROVERBS 10:9

It's right here in black and white what will happen in my life, according to which path I choose. I will admit I have been on both paths. The first one is a whole lot easier, smoother, and better.

November 10

Not only so, but we also glory in our sufferings, because we know that suffering produces perseverance; perseverance, character; and character, hope. And hope does not put us to shame, because God's love has been poured out into our hearts through the Holy Spirit, who has been given to us.
—ROMANS 5:3-5

I would try to figure out something happening in my life but couldn't. I had to give up and give it all to God. When I did my life turned what I thought was a negative into a positive. This built my perseverance, character, and hope.

November 11

My Father's house has many rooms; if that were not so, would
I have told you that I am going there to prepare a place for you?
And if I go and prepare a place for you, I will come back and
take you to be with me that you also may be where I am.
—JOHN 14:2-3

Jesus didn't lie. He told the truth. The human part of me still doubts what he is telling me in this scripture. I believe I don't deserve to live in such a wonderful place. I do believe it more today than I have ever have.

November 12

Let us draw near to God with a sincere heart and with the full assurance that faith brings, having our hearts sprinkled to cleanse us from a guilty conscience and having our bodies washed with pure water. Let us hold unswervingly to the hope we profess, for he who promised is faithful. And let us consider how we may spur one another on toward love and good deeds, not giving up meeting together, as some are in the habit of doing, but encouraging one another—and all the more as you see the Day approaching.
—HEBREWS 10:22-25

Life has its ups and downs. When all is good with my life someone else might be having a rough time. Through fellowship we learn about love, caring, and serving one another. We are taught through example about God. I have learned more about God since finding out I had cancer.

November 13

Splendor and majesty are before him; strength
and joy are in his dwelling place.
—1 CHRONICLES 16:27

God has everything I need.

November 14

Many of the Samaritans from that town believed in him because of the woman's testimony, "He told me everything I ever did!"
—JOHN 4:39

In spite of her past Jesus loved her. He gave her the gift none of us deserve, which shows me how much Jesus loves me.

November 15

I delight greatly in the Lord; my soul rejoices in my God. For he has clothed me with garments of salvation and arrayed me in a robe of his righteousness, as a bridegroom adorns his head like a priest, and as a bride adorns herself with her jewels.
—ISAIAH 61:10

I wear clothes to protect me from the worldly elements. A layer between me and the world. God clothes me in salvation and righteousness. The two qualities I need to live a peaceful and blessed life in this world.

November 16

For all of you who were baptized into Christ
have clothed yourselves with Christ.
—GALATIANS 3:27

My life was a total wreck. I was dependent on drugs, alcohol, and many other vices. It was an awful way to live.

I remember talking with a minister about God. I was baptized, and my whole family came to see their prayers being answered.

After my baptism I became sober and drug free. My life was totally turned around as I began my journey with Christ.

November 17

For everyone born of God overcomes the world. This is the
victory that has overcome the world, even our faith.
—1 JOHN 5:4

What is the definition of faith? Complete trust or confidence in someone or something—God. Our victory comes from God.

November 18

But blessed is the one who trusts in the
Lord, whose confidence is in him.
—Jeremiah 17:7

I trust in the Lord, and I am blessed. I didn't think this receiving the cancer diagnosis. Today, I consider myself blessed because my relationship with the Lord and others are stronger.

November 19

Your sun will never set again, and your moon will wane no more; the Lord will be your everlasting light, and your days of sorrow will end.
—ISAIAH 60:20

There are days on this earth when I have experienced the everlasting light of the Lord. I have the promise of knowing I will always be in his presence in Heaven. Heaven will always be.

November 20

And when you stand praying, if you hold anything
against anyone, forgive them, so that your Father
in heaven may forgive you your sins.
—MATTHEW 11:25

I wasn't even aware until someone pointed out to me the line in the Lord's Prayer, "forgive us our trespasses as we forgive those who trespass against us." Forgiveness comes to me as I forgive another at the same time.

November 21

The Spirit and the bride say, "Come!" And let the one who hears say, "Come." Let the one who is thirsty come; and let the one who wishes take the free gift of the water of life.
—REVELATION 22:17

I am so grateful because without the invitation I would have been destined to a life full of gloom and doom in the here and the hereafter.

November 22

*God is not human, that he should lie, not a human
being, that he should change his mind. Does he speak
and then not act? Does he promise and not fulfill?*
—NUMBERS 23:19

Everything the Bible has said about God has been true. I turned my will and life over to God. My life took a 360° turn for the better. It became smoother and easier even living with cancer.

November 23

But God demonstrates his own love for us in this:
While we were still sinners, Christ died for us.
—ROMANS 5:8

God knew we were human, and we were going to keep sinning in spite of ourselves. I have sinned when every core of my being was trying to do God's will. God sent his son to save us from ourselves. Thank you, God.

November 24

Therefore I do not run like someone running aimlessly; I do not fight like a boxer beating the air. No, I strike a blow to my body and make it my slave so that after I have preached to others, I myself will not be disqualified for the prize.
—1 Corinthians 9:26-27

A football player knows what is expected of him. I know God wants me to trust and have faith in him. Through him the cancer will be eradicated.

November 25

Set your minds on things above, not on earthly things.
—COLOSSIANS 3:2

I have to develop a habit of spiritual thinking and actions. My human nature wants me to be able to do the things on earth others are doing. This seems much easier, but just because it is easier doesn't mean it is better.

November 26

For who in the skies above can compare with the Lord?
Who is like the Lord among the heavenly beings?
—PSALM 89:6

There is none like the Lord. He is one of a kind. The Lord is our advocate and our intercessor. He is on our side. He is talking with God right now about this insidious disease of cancer.

November 27

For no word from God will ever fail.
—LUKE 1:37

God has done things in my life to humans seemed impossible. I am so grateful because I know God can annihilate this cancer just like he took care of the alcoholism and drug addiction in my life.

November 28

Then Jesus came to them and said, "All authority in heaven and on earth has been given to me."
—MATTHEW 28:18

Jesus came to earth as a human. He understands our human emotions, feelings, fears, and desires. This understanding enables him to plead our case to his Father.

*See, I have engraved you on the palms of my
hands; your walls are ever before me.*
—Isaiah 49:16

The Bible tells me God knows the number of hairs on my head. I am written in the Book of Life. My name is engraved on the palm of his hands, which is one of the places the nail was driven into when Jesus was crucified. He has me in his constant sight.

November 30

He died for us so that, whether we are awake or asleep, we may live together with him. Therefore encourage one another and build each other up, just as in fact you are doing.
—1 THESSALONIANS 5:10-11

We will be with Christ in the end. In the meantime, we need to encourage each other and build each other up. Why? I don't need any help with criticism from others. I do a pretty good job of that myself.

My friends and family have been by my side building me up and pushing me on living with cancer, and the treatments it involves.

December 1

*All Scripture is God-breathed and is useful for teaching, rebuking,
correcting and training in righteousness, so that the servant
of God may be thoroughly equipped for every good work.*
—2 TIMOTHY 3:16-17

The Bible is my guide for living. It has all the answers I need to live a relatively easy life. God's word helps me to live with the ups and downs of cancer.

December 2

Every good and perfect gift is from above, coming down from the Father of the heavenly lights, who does not change like shifting shadows.
—JAMES 1:17

God loves me so much he gives me gifts I don't deserve.

December 3

Therefore, as God's chosen people, holy and
dearly loved, clothe yourselves with compassion,
kindness, humility, gentleness and patience.
—Colossians 3:12

I have clothed myself with fear, hate, bigotry, malice, and jealously, which made living life difficult at best. I found compassion, kindness, humility, gentleness, and patience a much easier way to live.

I remember I would tell people, "There is good in all of us. Sometimes you just to have to look a little harder in others." Afterwards, I went through a stage where I didn't see much good in anyone.

Cancer has brought me back to believing there is some good in everyone.

December 4

And being found in appearance as a man, he humbled himself by becoming obedient to death—even death on a cross!
—PHILIPPIANS 2:8

Thank God he did this for me. If he hadn't, I would still be a lost and stumbling drunk with no hope.

December 5

*Religion that God our Father accepts as pure and faultless
is this: to look after orphans and widows in their distress
and to keep oneself from being polluted by the world.*
—JAMES 1:27

Specific instructions of how God wants me to live are what I need. They keep me from destroying my life. Today, I have to show up for treatments, and treat others as I want to be treated. God handles the rest.

December 6

After the earthquake came a fire, but the Lord was not
in the fire. And after the fire came a gentle whisper.
—1 KINGS 19:12

I had a tooth extracted. There was a bone fragment protruding where the tooth had been removed. I went back to the oral surgeon, and he pulled it out. It was an immediate relief. The fragment caused an annoying pain. I couldn't forget it was there.

The same is true with the Lord. His still small voice is powerful. When I listen to his voice. I know all will be well for me.

December 7

"No weapon forged against you will prevail, and you will refute every tongue that accuses you. This is the heritage of the servants of the Lord, and this is their vindication from me," declares the Lord.
—ISAIAH 54:17

When I realize my thinking is taking a negative turn. I have found the only way to change it is to say, "No weapon formed against me shall prosper, or in the name of Jesus Christ Satan get behind thee." I might have to say this off and on throughout the day.

There are days I feel like giving up and giving in. The scripture tells me the cancer won't prosper. Today, I will live my life the way God intended—helping others. My dark thinking then dissipates.

The Lord has done it this very day; let us rejoice today and be glad.
—PSALM 118:24

God has given me one more day to spread love, to put a smile on someone's face, to ask how someone is doing, to live by example, and to show the power of God.

Cancer wants me to be fearful, wants me to isolate, and wants me to give up. This isn't God's will. God has my life, and no one or disease can take me.

God is in charge of my life.

December 9

What, then, shall we say in response to these things?
If God is for us, who can be against us?
—ROMANS 8:31

Life can have a way of throwing a pitcher of ice, cold water in my face. God can and does work through other people. When the line is drawn in the sand God is always going to be on my side cheering me on and giving me the strength to put one foot in front of the other.

I am grateful I have cancer because without it I wouldn't have written this book. It doesn't mean I believe or feel this way all the time. The power of God is amazing.

December 10

No, in all these things we are more than conquerors through him who loved us. For I am convinced that neither death nor life, neither angels nor demons, neither the present nor the future, nor any powers, neither height nor depth, nor anything else in all creation, will be able to separate us from the love of God that is in Christ Jesus our Lord.
—Romans 8:37-39

A part of me had a problem with God sacrificing his only begotten son. We see a major tragedy, and people sacrifice their own lives to save others.

God sacrificed his son so many more lives could be saved. He knew beyond a shadow of a doubt Jesus was coming back to him, and his son would be living in eternal peace and love.

What a concept! God loves me this much. He loves you. Love is a powerful force. It can bring someone back to life. It washes away sins.

It has enabled me to live a life full of love in spite of the cancer.

December 11

Blessed are the merciful, for they will be shown mercy.
—MATTHEW 5:7

When I received the news of having cancer people brought food over to me and my family. They drove me to radiation, chemotherapy, doctor's appointments, and to AA meetings. They called to see if I needed anything.

I was shocked to see how many people actually cared about me. It renewed my faith in mankind. I was shown mercy though not deserving it.

Showing people mercy has been a result of painful experiences. Judging someone for an action they took, and then having the same experience. I realized we are doing the best we can. God feels the same way about us.

December 12

So do not fear, for I am with you; do not be dismayed,
for I am your God. I will strengthen you and help you;
I will uphold you with my righteous right hand.
—ISAIAH 41:10

This has been one of my most difficult areas in my life. Do I still have fears? Yes.

It was a new situation when I found out I had cancer. I began to look at the positive after focusing on the negative. I know God is always with me.

December 13

Praise the Lord, my soul, and forget not all his benefits—who forgives all your sins and heals all your diseases, who redeems your life from the pit and crowns you with love and compassion.
—Psalms 103:2-4

I know God has forgiven me. Am I still perfect? No. I am a lot better than I used to be.

I am utterly powerless living with cancer. God is with me in spirit and is in charge of my healing.

December 14

He heals the brokenhearted, and binds up their wounds.
—PSALMS 147:3

The day it was confirmed I had cancer my heart felt like it was breaking. All I could think about was missing my children, my grandchild, my husband, my family, and my friends. I didn't want to die or think about it. Wave after wave of fear was flooding through me, and I couldn't stop it.

I began trusting God, and my fear began to subside. God began healing my broken heart and binding up my wounds. My faith grew.

December 15

A cheerful heart is good medicine, but a
crushed spirit dries up the bones.
—PROVERBS 17:22

While receiving treatments on my lung and hip, I would wake up in the middle of the night, go into the living room, and turn on the television. Before long I would be crying after seeing a few depressing commercials or a program.

I was listening to a sermon, and the minister was talking about the healing power of laughter. How it produced endorphins. I began watching funny television shows and movies. This produced deep, hearty laughs.

I noticed my outlook on life, and my demeanor began slowly changing. I wasn't predicting gloom and doom. Life had become lighter. I call laughter God's natural medicine.

December 16

For God has not given us a spirit of fear, but of power and of love and of a sound mind.
—2 TIMOTHY 1:7

The fears attacked me with a vengeance with the cancer diagnosis. I was predicting the worse. For me one of the worst parts of having cancer is waiting on the results of a scan to see if there have been any improvements.

I learned from others who had cancer about staying in the moment, meditating, and flooding my mind with spiritual sermons or messages.

My morning continues to be filled with spiritual readings, journaling, and praying. God is my source.

December 17

Be strong and courageous. Do not be afraid or terrified because of them, for the Lord your God goes with you; he will never leave you nor forsake you.
—DEUTERONOMY 31:6

Jesus was in the Garden of Gethsemane. He knew what the outcome was going to be, but he was still scared. In this scripture Jesus taught me courage. He walked through the fear in spite of how he felt.

My life was ruled by fear, and it was an awful way to live. I slowly crawled out of the prison I had built myself. I still want to go back in there at times. I think it will be safe. In reality it's cold, dark, dank, tight, and confining. It's as if I am trapped.

I learned living life has the opposite effect. It's light, airy, freeing, open, and provides continuous enlightenment. I learned this through Jesus.

December 18

The LORD appeared to us in the past, saying: "I have loved you with an everlasting love; I have drawn you with unfailing kindness.
—JEREMIAH 31:3

God is always by my side, through thick and thin, better or worse, in sickness and in health. He is my best friend, parent, and spouse.

He doesn't change. His love is the same for me even when my circumstances change. He loved me when I didn't have cancer, and when I found out I did have cancer.

December 19

God is our refuge and strength, an ever-present help in trouble.
—PSALM 46:1

When the cancer was discovered I was in shock and tears. It moved to fear, and then to terror, gloom, and doom. I had to turn to God even when questioning him at the same time.

I spent more time with him studying his word and writing. He became a deeper part of my being. I took refuge in him. I was able to obtain the strength I needed for each day. My relationship with him deepened.

He is always there for me. "ALWAYS!!!"

December 20

The Lord is with me; I will not be afraid. What can man do to me? The Lord is with me; he is my helper.
—PSALM 118:6-7

I have found people, diseases, circumstances try to harm me in various ways, but the Lord is with me. He is by my side. He is going through this cancer with me. He won't leave me. He offers his help to me.

Who else would I want to help me or on my side, but the ultimate authority?

December 21

When I am afraid, I put my trust in you.
—PSALM 56:3

I tried all my human ways, means, schemes, and desires to fix my feelings. This failed, and I finally had to trust in a higher power.

I got tired of feeling sorry for myself because I had cancer, and wishing things were different. I had nothing left but to trust God, Jesus Christ, and the Holy Spirit—the trifecta.

December 22

Peace is what I leave with you; it is my own peace
that I give you. I do not give it as the world does. Do
not be worried and upset; do not be afraid.
—JOHN 14:27

Understanding I had cancer was a hard blow. I was terrified. I was panicky and questioned everything. I knew deep down within in my soul another human wasn't going to be able to give me lasting peace.

I gave up and surrendered again. It was the cancer and the treatments. The physical, mental, spiritual, and emotional abuse that comes with a cancer diagnosis.

I was at peace in spite of the fact nothing had changed about my disease. I knew everything was going to work out the way it was supposed to. I needn't be worried, upset, or afraid.

December 23

Do not be anxious about anything, but in every situation, by prayer and petition, with thanksgiving, present your requests to God. And the peace of God, which transcends all understanding, will guard your hearts and your minds in Christ Jesus.
—PHILIPPIANS 4:6-7

I realize not living in today can affect my heart and mind. Whenever I am anxious it's because I am trying to figure out a solution about the future.

The mornings are the worst time because it is harder for me to breathe, and my body aches all over. I have to guard my mind and heart. I let God take care of me, and I am at peace.

December 24

There is no fear in love. But perfect love drives out fear, because fear has to do with punishment. The one who fears is not made perfect in love.
—1 John 4:18

I let the negativity of life slowly seep into my being. It was all I focused on. It took a long time to change my thinking.

My cancer treatment plan would require me to arrange rides to radiation, chemotherapy, and meetings. My first thought. I don't have anyone who will want to take me. The next, I don't have any friends. I was so wrong.

The hard front I had built in order to protect myself began to crack and then to crumble. I found out people are full of love and are willing to show it. Their love drove out my fear and continues to do so.

When anxiety was great within me, your
consolation brought joy to my soul.
—Psalm 94:19

I had experienced more terror, panic, and feelings of abandonment before the cancer. I am not saying I didn't have feelings of confusion, sadness, and grief after the diagnosis. I had enough experience to know the feelings would pass.

God brought me great consolation and comfort. I had tried man, woman, child, food, cigarettes, alcohol, drugs, exercise, no exercise, and shopping. These were temporary and fleeting fixes.

I realized God is my source, and the healer of my anxiety.

December 26

But now, this is what the Lord says, "Fear not, for I have redeemed you; I have summoned you by name; you are mine."
—ISAIAH 43:1

I am the Lord's. I don't belong to anyone else. It might feel like someone is trying to summon me. The Lord has already redeemed me and has me.

An anxious heart weighs a man down,
but a kind word cheers him up.
—PROVERBS 12:25

The oncologist had a calming demeanor, but at the same time a take-charge confident attitude. He was honest, a great listener, but most importantly, he was kind. He had a kind and sincere soul. He was genuine.

It radiated from him, and I was instantly put at ease. My heart was lifted, and I became hopeful it was possible to live with cancer for years or even become cancer-free.

December 28

*Even though I walk through the valley of the shadow
of death, I will fear no evil, for you are with me;
your rod and your staff, they comfort me.*
—Psalm 23:4

I am protected by God through the use of his rod and staff. His rod protects me from the enemy. He uses his staff to keep me close to him. If we begin to stray away from him, he leads me back to where the power is.

December 29

Have I not commanded you? Be strong and courageous.
Do not be terrified; do not be discouraged, for the Lord
your God will be with you wherever you go.
—JOSHUA 1:9

I have been terrified and discouraged. It felt like I was in fear more than faith. I didn't feel the presence of God. It was an awful place for me to be.

I have to ask myself, "Was it really?"

Reflecting back, I learned so much during this time. My relationship with God grew deeper. I had to learn to ask for help from other people. I found. The more times I walked through fear. It became less and less.

December 30

Therefore do not worry about tomorrow, for tomorrow will worry about itself. Each day has enough trouble of its own.
—MATTHEW 6:34

I can do nothing about tomorrow. I can plan, usually something happens that I wasn't expecting, but it has always been for my good.

December 31

Humble yourselves, then, under God's mighty hand, so that he will lift you up in his own good time. Leave all your worries with him, because he cares for you.
—1 PETER 5:6-7

I don't know what is good for me. I always thought I did, but I learned God knows what is best for me. It's easier to humble myself because of my past experiences working out to my benefit. God cares for me.

CPSIA information can be obtained
at www.ICGtesting.com
Printed in the USA
BVHW081543020719
552496BV00001B/8/P